DALMORE TAILS

Donald John Maclennan

Illustrations by Archie B. Young

DEDICATION

To my granddaughter Amor
a light for the future

and to my uncles Iain and Murchadh Shoudie
an inspiration from the past

Also by Donald John Maclennan

Dalmore – Tales of a Lewis Village

ACKNOWLEDGMENTS

My sincere thanks go again to Les Ellingham who, in 2009, was responsible for taking my blog *Dalmore - Tales of a Lewis Village* from languishing on the internet to the written pages of a book.

With *Dalmore Tails*, Les once more took over the preparation and publishing of the book. His knowledge of matters relating to internet publishing and his advice was invaluable. He was sensitive to the nature of the stories and appreciated the vein of humour throughout them all. As with my first book, this one would not have been published without the total involvement of Les Ellingham and I thank him sincerely.

 Early on I approached my friend Archie Young to see if he could illustrate these stories, as photographs of a dog driving a motorbike must be impossible to find! Archie was Head of Art in my old school and I was delighted to see how easily he took to drawing these strange illustrations. Archie has a special humour which is evident in his drawings. We regularly fish Loch Awe together but I think he is better at his art!

 Finally, my thanks go to my son, Alasdair, and to Rosalinda for their unerring moral support and, above all, to the spectre of Iain Shoudie, whose nonsense tales live on in this book.

Donald John Maclennan

THE *TAILS*

THE CAST OF CHARACTERS

Iain Shoudie Dalmore's Doctor Dolittle. He could talk to the animals, as they could to him

Murdo Shoudie Iain's brother, had an exceptional memory and was a gifted story teller

Soho (aka So-Sally, Killy Soho) Sleek black cat, the alpha female in the house

Rupie A gentle female cat and Soho's close friend

Kenny Iceland An old moth eaten tomcat who hunted the rabbit warrens

Stowlia A female sheepdog, in name only, but wise and faithful

Shonnie Glass Formerly at sea, now a budding business man in the district

Dollag (Dolly) Shonnie's sister, a kindly lady, who ran the house

Filax A beautiful female tabby cat, content to stay close to the house

Fancy Shonnie's female sheepdog, who will travel anywhere at any time with Shonnie on the motorbike

Tom the Cat (Tom RNR, Tom Warrener) A ratter in the Navy ships, who like Kenny, preferred to hunt the hills.

Victoria (Vicky) A beautiful blue-cream Persian cat. She expected to be treated as a lady

Jura A black Labrador, she was wise and gentle and the other animals looked up to her

Fred A feisty and highly intelligent Parson Russell Terrier. A great character, he was fearless and extremely fast on any terrain.

In Dalmore

Some People Talk to the Animals

In the Highlands and Islands of Scotland, a belief in apparitions and spectres (Gael. *Tannaisg)* was almost universal in the past, and it would be a brave soul who would rubbish these ghost stories after leaving a black house on a moonless night to make his or her way home. Many of the stories told around the peat fire in that ceilidh house would send shivers up and down your spine. Rigid with fear, it was better to feign belief in ghosts till you reached home. A few people have always been endowed with the ability to see or hear these spirits and, of them, some failed to understand the torment of these tortured souls. It might take a hundred years or more for another person to finally lay the spirit to rest. In Lewis there were people who were gifted (some might say cursed) in their ability to 'see into the future'. We call such a person a 'seer', while in Gaelic he was known as *fear fiosaiche*, literally 'one who knows'. The most celebrated Highland seer was reputedly born long ago in Baile na Cille, in the parish of Uig in Lewis. His name was Kenneth Mackenzie, *Coinneach Odhar* or *Coinneach Fiosaiche*. I have known some people from our own district who, by repute, possessed this 'gift'.

There is another gift, and very rare it is, which is bestowed on some people. This is the ability to talk to animals and to put themselves out there, to listen to them with the same patience and understanding which we proffer to our fellow man. From the days of St. Francis of Assisi we harbour a deep desire to believe that animals can speak and that there are people who can understand what the animals are saying and so respond in kind. You can, if you like, call this anthropomorphism, where we attribute to animals the personality and feelings of mankind. But in truth, there are a rare few who can speak to the animals, people who can respond to a dog's bark, understand the insistent mews of a cat, or appreciate the whinny of the old grey mare.

As a young boy in Dalmore, a beautiful village on the west coast of the Isle of Lewis, I was privileged to know one such 'Dr. Dolittle', for the want of a better title. 'Iain Shoudie', my uncle John Maclennan, was that man, truly gifted in the art of animal talk. His brother, Murdo ('Murchadh') had this power also but to a lesser extent. They lived at No.4 Dalmore, a *taigh dubh* located high above the road, nestling under the *beinn*. These two brothers were my father's older siblings, unhurried, unmarried, and as happy as the day was long - no hurry, no worry. In harmony with each other (well, most of the time), they were at one with nature and in commune with their animals. As time goes by, we will be privy to the conversations and thoughts of So-Sally, Rupie, Stowlia and Kenny Iceland, just a few of the animals who shared *Taigh Shoudie* with the 'boys'.

Stay with us to hear what these animals and their friends had to share with Iain and Murdo. You might not believe it, but it is all true ('An 'Houdie told me so).

Coinneach Odhar - Kenneth of sallow complexion

taigh dubh - traditional thatched house

beinn – hill

Taigh Shoudie – Iain Shoudie's house

Bha Soho agus Rupie a' Comhradh
(Having a Cat Chat)

Darkness had just fallen on Dalmore. As always, the roar of the Atlantic rollers could be heard hitting the wide sandy beach down at the *traigh*. The ever present west wind was strong, and hurried the rain directly up the glen which is Dalmore (Gael. *dail mor*). Even at the Mullach Mor, about half a mile out, you could taste the salt in the raindrops which passed your lips. Weather like this was not unknown in the *dailean*.

High up on croft number 4, a single yellow light could be seen, but only with difficulty could one make out the outline of the long *taigh dubh*, directly under the *beinn*. On a night like this, the light coming through that single skylight was comfort indeed to any passing stranger. Inside this house of thick walls and thatched roof, it was warm, and the illumination came from a single 100 watt bulb, when before it would have come from the glowing mantle of the Tilley lamp. The two boys (the 'men' in the house) were having a wee *norrag* to themselves. Murchadh had lain down his book and his bendy, rimless 'spegligans' and was fast asleep sitting by the fire, his back to the dresser and his head leaning against the wall. By the way, 'spegligans' is not the Gaelic for spectacles, although one might think so, it is one of the word corruptions used in this house, baffling to some, but appreciated by the initiated. Iain was stretched out on the *being*, sleeping soundly, his head resting on his rolled-up bib overalls.

The peat fire was burning nicely between the stacks, radiating a warm heat. Sitting close to each other, with their eyes half-shut, almost hypnotised by the flicker of the yellow flame, sat So-Sally and Rupie, the resident cats in *Taigh Shoudie.* As the 'boys' slept, Soho and Rupie would discuss matters concerning only themselves, without Old Dolittle giving 'fatherly advice'. After all, there were certain cat issues which were easier to discuss on their own, without the distractions of man or dog. Occasionally they would hold their front *spogain* up to the fire to toast their pads, something they had seen the 'boys' do. You may have noticed that Killy-Soho will have a few name changes in a pretty short time (i.e. So-Sally, Soho). This was the doing of Iain Shoudie, who was wont to play around with words and names, just as one finds the names changing so disconcertingly in the Russian Novel.

Soho: "Isn't this just nice, now, *A'Ghraidh*. Listen to the sound of the wind whistling through the thatch and the rain hitting the window pane. We have a good home here, Rupie, and we are very fortunate that the 'boys' can speak our language and understand us. It makes life so much easier for all concerned."

Soho was the alpha female by dint of age and experience and, when required, had demonstrated well honed fighting skills, but not among her own household, to be sure. She was sleek, with a very shiny black coat, and moved like a miniature panther. She liked mankind, but was not so keen on dogs, unless she got a nod of approval from the 'boys' for a visiting dog. Julia, the resident dog, was obviously an exception, and if truth to be told, she loved Stowlia to bits (Stowlia, a patronymic for Julia).

Rupie: "You are right, So-Sally. We have a good home here, and Iain and Murdo are so kind. I am glad we can have this wee chat while the others are asleep. Last week, in the morning, I accompanied Murchadh (Murdo) as he took the cows out to their usual pastures, over the other side of the Beinn. On the way, Stowlia and I listened to Murdo regale us with some old Gaelic proverbs. He is good at the proverbs, but some of them I've heard a few times now! I was feeling very happy, and content to let Stowlia lead through the tall heather. When Murdo stopped at Loch Dubh na Cleit to water the cattle and have himself a cigarette, I decided to strike out on my own and bade farewell to them both as I headed down the Cleit towards Dalbeg. I had never been as far from home before, and this would be a new experience for me. And yet I felt that old Stowlia was uneasy at me going to Dalbeg on my own. As I descended from the Cleit, I reached the edge of the Village Loch, beautiful in its massive show of white water-lilies. In what spaces there were between the extensive floating lily rafts, brown trout made many 'rises', some clearing the water completely in a great show of acrobatics.

Dail Beag is *Dail Mor's* wee sister, and some would attest to its greater beauty. I was crossing high above the little golden beach along a rabbit run, when a little ahead of me I saw something which made me freeze to the spot. There, dead ahead was a very large male mink, bigger than any I'd seen at George Macleod's mink farm in Dalmore. Long, with a black glossy coat, this animal had escaped from an island mink farm, and looked good on it. Those who bred the mink never acknowledged that it could be a farm escapee. Old Archie used to say that, in that case, they must have flown in from North America by plane."

Mink are ferocious killers, deadly in their entrapment of prey, and if free to roam at will, they will wreak havoc with nesting birds, rabbits and domestic fowl. Rupie did not move a muscle as she observed the mink's nose twitch below a pair of beady red eyes. Rupie had only ever seen mink behind the secure mesh of a cage, but here out in the open she had no idea what this big mink might do. Her wee heart was pounding against her rib cage, and she could only hope that the mink would not notice. Then the strangest of things! The mink looked Rupie straight in the eye, climbed unhurriedly out of the rabbit run and vanished into a field of hay. As soon as she realised her good luck, there was a massive adrenaline rush which carried Rupie at speed around Loch Dalbeg, and up the hill to the safety of the Cleit. Soho, that wise old cat, was sitting outside No.4, as was Stowlia the dog, when Rupie arrived home. Stowlia was a little upset with Rupie, and only shook her head when they met. Soho asked Rupie in a quiet voice to sit down beside her. She asked her about her solo trip to Dalbeg, and cautioned her against repeating this 'adventure' again on her own.

Soho: "Rupie, did you realise how concerned we would be about you? As bad as that meeting with the mink was, it could have been so much worse if it had been a female mink, especially if her young had been close by. The female is much smaller than the male mink, but in agility and speed it is fearsome. It might not have attacked you, but had it done so, you, Rupie, were in mortal danger. Please, *A' Ghraidh*, always say where you are going, and if it's out of sight of home, make sure that I or Stowlia are with you." Rupie nodded agreement, and Stowlia gave her a warm smile.

The Shoudie Boys had just awakened from their 'forty winks'. Murdo threw a couple of peats on the fire, and the old black kettle was put on to boil for their *copan teatha*. All was hunky dory once more, the more so because Kenny Iceland, their hill cousin had 'come in from the cold' and was warming himself *aig an teine*.

Murdo was knowledgeable about the history of these parts, and had this to say to his small assembled audience, which included his brother John who knew less about history and more about humourous ditties and nonsense rhymes.

Murdo: "We must not forget that not so long ago, around 1750, the Isle of Lewis was a lawless and dangerous place, where the rule of law had hardly taken root and any religious awakening would have to wait some seventy years. It was in such times that an awful incident occurred in the bay at Dalbeg. A tall sailing ship known as a clipper was shipwrecked during the night on the large rocks at the Ard on the northern side of the bay, during a furious storm. Its cargo was mainly tea, held in hundreds of chests, which were destroyed on the rocks. Witnesses said that the seas in Dalbeg Bay were now a deep brown colour. The piles of tea leaves heaped on the shore were later gathered by the villagers and spread on their *feannagain*, thinking it a good fertiliser. It was said that nothing grew on that ground for quite a few years. The men of Dalbeg were not there to save lives or to show mercy to those sailors struggling ashore. They were there for booty and plunder. Those poor souls who reached the beach were slaughtered as they lay there. Others of the crew, who could see what was happening, attempted to climb the high cliffs to reach the Ard. Those who made it to the top were systematically murdered, usually by chopping their hands off at the cliff's edge. One man is said to have escaped that night with only one hand, the other having been amputated, but not before putting a curse on the village, a curse which has never been raised. Remembering that Dalbeg (Gael. *Dail Beag*) means 'small dale or valley', the sailor said:

'Dalbeg, as small as you are now, you will be even smaller in times to come. No grandfather will ever see a grandchild born during his lifetime'.

And to this day, that has been the case in Dalbeg, Rupie. Dalbeg is a very strange place."

traigh – beach or shore

dail mor - big dale

dailean – the dales of Dalmore and Dalbeg

norrag – forty winks

being - bench

Taigh Shoudie - the Shoudie Boys' house

spogain – paws

A'Ghraidh - my dear

Dail Beag - small dale

copan teatha - cup of tea

aig an teine - at the fire

feannagain - strip fields

The Gang of Five Picnic on the Traigh

It was a truly beautiful morning. The sun shone bright and warm, with only a few wisps of cloud to be seen in the blue above the horizon. The view from the door of the old *taigh dubh* at No.4 was as beautiful as anyone could imagine. Your eyes took in the *feannaigan* of corn and potatoes, and were inexorably drawn to the golden sands of Dalmore beach. There was a very light breeze and the waves in the bay were shallow and barely audible as they reached shore. It was not always like this. In winter huge waves could be seen to break through the cemetery wall, and tidal floods would rush all the way up the *allt*.

But today was different. The house animals of *Taigh Shoudie* were sitting or lying on the grassy *leathad* in front of the house. It was going to be a glorious day, and one did not need the BBC to confirm this forecast. You just had to study the wave activity out at Rudha 'an Trilleachain to determine the weather for that day. Iain Shoudie sat beside his three friends, smoking a roll-up and drinking strong tea from a mug. Cigarettes bought in packets, he called 'ready mades'. They were like smoking a page of the Gazette, he would say. But when he ran out of Rizla papers, then a page of the 'Cassette' it would have to be. So-Sally, Rupie and Stowlia would occasionally turn round to look at Iain, who guessed what might be in their minds.

Iain: "What a beautiful morning, ladies. All the chores are done, and it would be a shame to waste the day up here, when a picnic down at the *traigh* would be just the thing".

Notwithstanding the weather, the animals could picnic any day they liked, as there never were any chores to do in *Taigh Shoudie*, not even for the 'boys'.

So-Sally: "That's a grand idea, Iain, and it would be even better if Filax and Fancy were invited. They are so nice and such good company. Rupie, would you mind nipping over to *Taigh Glass* at No.5 and letting them know about the picnic this afternoon."

"Right away", said wee Rupie.

Filax and Fancy were the cat and dog who stayed with Shonnie and Dollag in the beautiful *taigh dubh* on the opposite side of the glen. They (i.e. the animals) were an easy going pair, on whom you could always rely. The Glass and Shoudie animals had historically been close friends. Filax was a well-fed brown and white tabby cat who generally stuck close to the house but she was delighted at the thought of a picnic with her good friends, the Shoudies. Fancy, the dog, had gone up to the shop in Carloway riding pillion behind Shonnie on the motorbike. Dollag expected them back soon.

Back soon, they were. Fancy jumped off the pillion seat, and the Shoudie trio did well to stifle their laughter at Fancy's new get-up. She greeted them all with a smile on that bonnie sonsie face of hers. Over her head with the ears tucked in, Fancy was wearing a brown leather flying helmet and some snazzy aviator's glasses.

"Well, what do you think?" enquired Fancy.

"O, *A'Ghraidh*, you look the part!", said Stowlia, her face frozen in the rictus of a smile.

Filax: "Annie in Renfrew got a job lot of American airforce surplus in a large store in Glasgow. What her boys can't (or won't) wear, she sent home here to Dalmore. Don't you think Fancy looks the bees' knees in that get-up? She will be the talk of the district"

Rupie: "*Se sinn a'firinn!* "

The 'Gang' would be well provided with victuals. There were some saithe and cuddies left over from lunch at the 'boys' table. Iain had caught them at Banderberie and they had been fried in this morning's bacon fat. Milk and cream, boiled potatoes and some 'grey' soup completed their picnic 'hamper'.

Down at the *traigh*, Fancy and Stowlia played their usual game of 'pursuits', in and out of the small waves, making sure they stepped over every little roller which approached (bad luck if you didn't). After that, they made their way out to where the waves were taller, and, diving in, they allowed the surf to carry them back to shore. It was great sport and one which just might catch on in time.

Soho and Rupie were encouraging Filax to dip her *spogs* in the *allt*. Although this is normally anathema to cats, there are circumstances when a cat must brave the waters and, if they were to dam the river, then they would have to take onboard a little water. But surfing the waves like Stowlia and Fancy was a no-no, of course. In the end, more than their *spogs* were wet, but that didn't dampen their spirits.

After a tasty repast, they all decided to go up river to where Allt Dhail a' Mor emerges from Lot a' Bhoer in order to start the Boat Race. This would be the highlight of the afternoon, when Mrs. Tunnag and her brood of ducklings would play such an important part in the proceedings. In times past the boats were simply small pieces of driftwood, but oft times in the course of a race, boats would maroon themselves on the bank or behind some obstacle. Now, of course, five little ducklings, with Mother Tunnag's blessing, presented themselves at the start line as self propelled river jockeys, each bearing the favour of one of the 'Gang of Five'. As the race progressed, the excitement was palpable, and more than once a bit of shoving, ducking, and diving was observed. Fancy stated that it was the taking part that was important, but the dishevelled wee bundle of feathers that crossed the line ahead of the rest was having none of that Olympic nonsense.

After a celebratory dinner, everyone made their way home, very tired but very happy. They resolved to do the same again, some other day.

allt - small river

leathad - slope

Rudha 'an Trilleachain - Oyster Catchers' point

Taigh Glass – Glass's house

"Se sinn a'firinn!" - that's for sure!

spogs – paws

A New Recruit
Tom the Cat RNR (Royal Naval Ratcatcher)

World War Two was all but over, when Shonnie was drafted to a small naval vessel at Devonport on the south west coast of England. It was there he first clapped eyes on Tom, who was weaving his way through the legs of the sailors in their mess, picking up a morsel here and there. This big tomcat had attitude and his sailor 'oppos' had great affection for the big fella. A ratter of extraordinary ability, no one can recall ever seeing any vermin below decks. Tom (no time for fancy nancy names in the Navy) had been a member of the crew for a few years now, and was a source of comfort to the men, eager to return home to Blighty. They had a small sailor's hat made for him, with navy blue ribbons which tied under his chin. Tom was proud of the honour his crew mates had bestowed on him and, when the mess table had been cleared, he would parade on top, tail held high and erect as a poker; he moved with the prancing steps of a Lipizzaner horse. There was much cheering and laughter which further encouraged our thespian moggy to reprise. Shonnie could not believe his eyes, the more so when some of the crew began singing 'The Drunken Sailor'. When it came to the chorus, 'Hooray and Up He Rises', Tom would rise up on his back *spogs* ever so gingerly, sway with the music, and punch the air with his two remaining paws. Grown men were seen to weep with laughter. The captain was a frequent visitor to this floor show below decks.

How Shonnie managed to adopt Tom when he left the Navy I don't know, but home together they came to Dalmore in 1946. Shonnie gave Tom a glowing testimony to his father, Bodach Glass, and his two sisters, explaining how fortunate they were to have exclusive use of the greatest rat catcher in His Majesty's Senior Service. They were much impressed. Tom was himself impressed with his new home in the glen, a far cry from his former station among the darkness, the dirt, and the smell of the ship's bilges. Here were high hills and fertile fields, a place where, in the past, he could only dream about. There may be some rats in the roof space of No. 5, his new home, but if he were not mistaken (and he wasn't) he

could count a dozen or so rabbits leaping about the hill with impunity. He would need to renegotiate his contract with Shonnie, which he did, on the understanding that he would tutor the resident cats in the best practices of ratting.

This was indeed a home fit for heroes.

Aig Reitich an a' Siabost

It is always an occasion on the island when two cats decide to marry because, in truth, it doesn't happen very often and hardly ever in Shawbost. Uisdean (Hugh) was from Upper Carloway, a fine big ginger tom (there's those Norse genes again) and Eilidh (Helen) was from New Shawbost, her hair almost all white, with a neat little pink nose and a rear right *spog* of charcoal black. Eilidh and Uisdean were third cousins, who had known each other for some time now, and we all thought that if there was to be a cat wedding in our lifetime, then it would be theirs.

Soho and Rupie had invitations to the wedding, through friendship or kinship, while Kenny, *'Cat a' bheinn'* was persuaded to tag along, having come down from the creeks for a spell. Anyway he might just find a *brammer* there, although rabbits were really his thing, if you get what I mean. Now this wasn't the wedding as such that they would be going to, but the *reitich,* which in the Hebrides is an event celebrating the betrothal of the couple about to marry. Relatives and close friends of Eilidh and Uisdean were invited to the *reitich* to celebrate their forthcoming nuptials. There was a great deal of cat cleaning going on in *Taigh Shoudie* that afternoon. *Spogs* and rasping tongues were very busy, and old Murchadh Shoudie had to smile as he watched Rupie trying to lick a centre parting into the forehead of a strangely shy Kenny Iceland. Murchadh (Murdo) placed a piece of broken mirror against a table leg for the ladies to take a look, and off the three Shoudie cats went, laughing and cavorting as they climbed up the *beinn.*

As they descended the Cleit into Dalbeag, they encountered a worthy lady of the village known as *'Banntrach Cu Aonghas Dhubh'*. This was a lengthy moniker for anyone to carry, but this old lady dog revelled in her name because of her love for her recently departed husband, that is to say - departed this earth and not up the road to Shawbost. Her Gaelic name tells us that she is the widow of Black Angus' dog. She was rightly proud of her husband's action a few years back, when villagers witnessed his brave rescue of a young child who was being carried away from the beach by a strong rip tide. His name was Ben, and his dear widow was named *Sine*. When they were together, she was known as *'Beinn Ben Aonghas'*- literally 'the wife of Angus' Ben'.

Skirting the beautiful beach of *Dail Beag*, they climbed the *leathad* and arrived at the northern side of Loch Raoinavat, below Cregan Loch an Iaruinn where, in the past, the ancients built a circle of stones which now lie flat in the rough grass. They moved at speed now to the other end of the loch, whose waters join Allt na Breac which powers the old mill further down the river. Here they joined the road into Shawbost. They were looking forward to the *reitich* of their good friends, Eilidh and Uisdean, two of the nicest 'cat people' you could ever know. 'Cat people' was what Iain Shoudie called cats that spoke to humans. They didn't have to, of course, and some chose not to. As they neared the village, they saw some large crows sitting on a fence who greeted them courteously enough, but from behind a *cruach mhoine* appeared an altogether different crow, a black feathered, big beaked guy whom you would not normally see *air a' Taobh Siar*.

He was wearing a narrow brimmed leather cap, pulled low down over one eye, and a multicoloured scarf around his skinny neck, weighed down by a large metal cross. He stood there in the middle of the road, his legs akimbo, leaning back at a pronounced angle and with one wing of shiny black feathers fully stretched and pointing downwards, he muttered "Yo, man, what's going down? Where yo beeches goin'?". Well, the Dalmore group had never seen or heard anything like this anywhere before, although, if it were to happen anywhere, Shawbost would be high on the list. One of the other crows apologised for his 'friend's' bizarre behaviour, and our party continued towards New Shawbost, unmolested but a little bemused. Later that night, they learned a little from Eilidh about this manic crow. She knew his people well. "*Broinein bochd*", she whispered in low tones, which just about says it all! "It seems that he once flew out to Glasgow to stay with cousins in White Street in Partick, and was never the same again. He sits around all day chewing straw, and listening to 'rat music'. He's really a nice crow, just different. His friends look after him."

Soho, Rupie and Kenny Iceland had a wonderful time at the *reitich*. There were lots of cats there (naturally) but not exclusively. They noticed Toss and Tiny, those two Carloway canine worthies in the barn giving it big licks during a 'Strip the Willow'. The food was very tasty and the bowls of cream kept coming. Everyone raised their *spog* held glasses to the future happiness of Eilidh and Uisdean. As they made their way home in the early hours, the full moon lit up their path as if it were daylight. They had to agree that there were some very nice people in Shawbost, albeit they were descended from the *Lochlannich* (Norsemen). They had lots to tell the 'boys', Murdo and John, back in Dalmore.

> *Cat a' bheinn* - hill cat
>
> *brammer* – girlfriend (perhaps Gaelic)
>
> *Sine* – Jane
>
> *cruach mhoine* - peat stack
>
> *air a' Taobh Siar* - on the west side
>
> *Broinein bochd* - 'poor sick person'

THE RT. REV. MACCOLLIE
MINISTERS TO THE ANIMALS

One would never think that our friends, the animals, could have religious beliefs. However, about this, a paradox has always existed. Noah was commanded to save the animals in the Great Flood, and yet we are told in scripture that there will be no room for earth's animals in the heavens above. Not a little bird falls to the ground, we are told, that Heaven does not know about. These contradictions, and some more, have, since time began, forced the animals to play it safe and follow mankind in their numerous religious beliefs. All over the world, the religious practices of their masters, are mirrored in those of their animals e.g. Hindu/Hindu or Buddhist/Buddhist etc.

In *Taigh Shoudie*, Murdo and Iain were nominally Church of Scotland, but their attendance at services was almost nil. But the 'boys' were almost uniquely aware that the animals might have religious leanings and, because of that, they were encouraged to attend church, if they so desired. Dogs and cats were adherents of the Animal Church in Scotland, by far the largest in the country. There were now many foreign breeds of dog and cat in the Church, but this church was all-inclusive and that, everyone believed, was a good thing. Services and prayer meetings were held in an old abandoned house in Doune, down by the loch, and these were generally well attended. The human population would not be aware of these large gatherings, which commenced at 3.00 am. on Sunday mornings, and mankind seemed deaf to the baying and eldritch shrieks of the animals in their Psalm singing. A big attraction at the Animal Church in Scotland here in Doune was undoubtedly the minister in charge, the Right Reverend John MacCollie, an evangelical and possessed of the 'charismatic', some professed.

This huge dog had very humble beginnings. In his testimony, he speaks of his first memory being with his two brothers, all three of them pups, at the 'Cat and Dog Home' in Cardonald

in Glasgow. This was not an auspicious start in life but, as a minister here in Lewis, he now occupied a position of respect among the people at large. Rev. MacCollie was a humble man, *'eagalach diadhaidh'*, people said. He was converted during one of the many 'awakenings' that had swept through the island in times past. His master took the *curam* and Big John MacCollie followed in his wake.

The Dalmore animals, with a few exceptions (the hill cats, Tom and Kenny Iceland), were fairly regular attendees on Sundays but rarely went to the Wednesday prayer meetings, which were for the truly committed and the *curamach*. In any case it was a fair distance down to Doune. The Precentor, who leads the congregation in singing the Psalms, but never, ever hymns, was an old grey moggy, called *'Donnachadh Spagach'*. Old Duncan was an irascible old tom, who started every psalm with the tune of 'Amazing Grace', irrespective of the psalm that had been called. Talk of caterwaulin! Old Duncan's 'singing' was a painful experience for those, like Fancy and Rupie, who knew every psalm by heart and enjoyed singing.

The Right Reverend MacCollie (the title Rt. Rev. was conferred on him for being Moderator of the General Assembly of the Animal Church in Scotland in 1950) was a humble big soul who felt a little awkward when addressed as the Right Reverend by any one of his congregation. During the week, he was like any other crofter's dog, whether at a *fank* or at the peats. There was however one thing which puzzled other animals about John MacCollie, and So-Sally was definitely one of them. No matter where he went, or the work he was involved in, MacCollie always wore his dog collar, whether grappling with sheep or cutting peat out on the moor. For such a humble dog, others could not understand the ever present dog collar. He seemed to be very attached to it. Well, in a way he was.

For the Dalmore crowd, it was time to return home, but there would be no singing or laughing, as it was still the Sabbath. Someone once 'reported' Soho and Rupie for just that and Iain Shoudie was very cross with them - well, not really. He just shook his head, gave a wink and smiled.

> *eagalach diadhaidh* - terribly godly
>
> *curam* - conversion
>
> *curamach* – converted
>
> *'Donnachadh Spagach'* - hen-toed
>
> *fank* – a pen for enclosing sheep

A Doll Dhachaidh
(Going Home)

For Dalmore's cats and dogs, the summer months of July and August were always eagerly anticipated. This was when the Islanders from every part of Britain would return 'home' to the village of their birth; *'leis na'daoine againn-fhein'* (with our own people). Often, they would bring with them their 'pets', a strange name mainlanders had for their animals, but perhaps not so when you observed the miscellany of creatures that descended on Lewis. Rupie asked Murdo about 'pets', but was none the wiser for his explanation. She was to learn much later, that the only time one would hear this word was if Iain Shoudie had to hand feed a young lamb whose mother had died, or had 'not taken to' her lamb. Bottle fed in the house, such a hand reared creature was called a 'pet lamb'. In no other sense was the word 'pet' used with regards to animals, as far as I know. Pets or not, these strange cats and dogs were like a breath of fresh air in the village and many were the friendships that were forged between Dalmore's animals and the mainland 'crew'. Among many of the cats and dogs it was a case of renewed friendship, as the majority of the *Gall* had been in Dalmore before.

The regular visitors to Nos. 4 and 5 Dalmore were free to stay in either house, which they regularly did. Prominent among them was Victoria Chantelle, a blue-cream Persian cat, the epitome of feline beauty, who hated her pedigree second name, Chantelle, which she thought sounded like that yellow mushroom favoured by chefs. Blue-cream was fine but yellow, no. She was always called Vicky, except on the odd formal occasion she attended with Mr. Dow, her boyfriend. Vicky's grown daughter, by Mr. Dow of course, was a beautiful large tabby with a white front and white *spogs* on an otherwise striped fur coat. She was a very bonnie cat, with a delightful nature. She answered to 'Tigger'. Bringing up the rear, so to speak, was Guinness, 'the Cardonald Cat', a small slim black cat with white markings on her mouth and *spogs*. She did not enjoy any mention of Cardonald, unlike the Reverend MacCollie who never failed to mention that place in every testimony he gave. In charge of these holiday cats was Jura, the black Labrador who had travelled up with her 'three sisters' from Glasgow by 'train and Macbrayne' (their little joke). It should be pointed out that their master accompanied them, since the rail and boat authorities had some strict rules vis-à-vis animals in transit. Jura would venture that these companies might take a closer look at the state of the poor *craturs* that stumble in and out of that favoured room, the 'saloon bar'. Still, they were so happy to be 'home' once more in Dalmore, with all their 'cousins'.

Tigger and Jura mostly stayed at No.5 with Filax and Fancy. Tigger and Filax looked alike, and were simply two of the gentlest of creatures - what you might say, 'real pussycats'. Fancy and Jura were straight out of Burns' poem, *The Twa Dogs:*

Jura

Her hair, her size, her mouth, her lugs,

Shew'd she was nane o'Scotland's dogs,

But whalpet some place far abroad,

Where sailors gang to fish for Cod

Burns here is describing a Labrador dog, or it might be a Newfoundland dog. Same difference, I'd say!

Fancy

The tither was a ploughman's collie,

A rhyming, ranting, raving billie.

Her gawsie tail, wi' upward curl,

Hung owre her hurdies wi' a swirl

No explanation needed here, except that the original dogs in Burns's poem, Caesar and Luath were male, and

Nae doubt but they were fain o'ither

Victoria Chantelle (sorry, Vicky) that beautiful blue-cream Persian cat boldly stated that she would reside only at No.5, a modern *taigh dubh* cared for by two maiden ladies, a house beautifully appointed with dressers, settees, fireside chairs, curtains and some *wally dugs*. As nice as the Shoudie Boys were, and even if they could talk to the animals, Vicky couldn't see herself spending eight weeks up the hill at No.4 - no way, *a' ghraidh*!

Guinness always knew where she would stay; up the *leathad* at *Taigh Shoudie* with So-Sally, Rupie and Stowlia the dog and Kenny Iceland, if he was actually 'in from the cold'. It might be a tad primitive (two old bachelors) but this was a house full of fun, music and ceilidh. Iain Shoudie was the Master of Ceremonies in this theatre of laughter, because all agreed that Iain was best placed to talk to, and to understand, the animals. You might recall that *'an Shoudie* was, if you like, 'Dalmore's Doctor Dolittle' possessing a very rare gift shared to a lesser extent with his brother Murchadh (Murdo).

Gall – strangers

craturs – creatures

wally dugs - Glaswegian for Staffordshire Pottery Dogs

How Did The Romans
Get Into Our Story?

Three cats and a black labrador dog from a city suburb have exchanged the home comforts of their neat estate semi for a wild glen on the west coast of Lewis in the Outer Hebrides. Here in the village of Dalmore, their home for the coming weeks' will be the *taighean dubha* of their animal 'cousins', houses built with walls six feet thick and with thatched roofs, in which man, cows and other sundry animals are housed under the one roof. The contrasts between the city and their holiday destination could not be more stark.

During their time in Britain, the islands in the far north and west, such as the Hebrides, were known to the Romans by the designation, 'Ultima Thule'; literally the 'ends of the earth'. With a gale blowing and the rains in from the sea in mid-July, the Romans understandably did not tarry long exploring these densely forested, unforgiving islands. There is however some evidence (coins, pottery shards) that the Romans attacked some brochs on the west coast but this was probably no more than a bit of lively action, ballista practice for their soldiers, in order to alleviate the boredom. So-Sally wondered how the 'bloody' Romans (Latin. cum sanguine) got into this story which the animals thought had been going so well. Fine, so it's back to Dalmore!

The total tally of tails (so to speak), all the cats and dogs in *Taigh Glass* and *Taigh Shoudie*, had agreed to meet this morning, with a view to some adventure, but only if it were dry (cats don't do rain). It was dry, with the sun promising to show. Some of the other cats and dogs in Dalmore often joined this troop, but unfortunately I cannot recall their names. These happy souls met that first morning on *liathad Shoudie* (the grassy slope outside No.4) and as they passed in the road towards the *traigh*, it was obvious the form their adventure would take. Whether man or beast, everyone always spent their first morning on Dalmore's famous golden strand. On their way in the road they laughed and played, happy to be in each other's company again. By now the sun was out and a few wispy clouds were gently moving across the sky, encouraged by a very light breeze. One could be excused for using the word 'Caribbean' to describe the warm, balmy, morning on Dalmore beach. The tide was well out but Fancy, Stowlia and Jura, our 'ladydogs' reached the small waves that rippled past their *spogs* only to die away. Floating in the sea further out were bundles of different seaweeds, which powerful waves had torn from the rocks in recent stormy weather. Our Dalmore dogs did a few tastings for Jura to show how tasty and nourishing some seaweeds could be. Jura's favourite was the beautiful red fronds of what is locally called *duileasg* - nice and crunchy, and reputedly full of iron and iodine which they say are 'good for you'. They headed much further out and went crashing into the high waves, which inevitably carried them back in. They coughed and spluttered and laughed, but they were happy, as happy as ever a dog could be.

The 'ladycats' were engrossed in things on the drier stretches of the *traigh*, where there were large areas of salt water pools left behind by the receding tide. There were a number of jelly fish, which Vicky, Tigger and Guinness had never encountered before, and whose dangers were explained by their country cousins. Still, Guinness tentatively touched one with a *spog*, which drew a rebuke from Tigger, her self-appointed 'mother'. There were many other things that the sea had jettisoned on the beach, which were quite safe to examine, and that included a dead sea bird. Unpleasant as this was, it was unlikely to sting you. The dead bird was covered in sand and small jumping flies, and it proved to be an interesting anatomical specimen for our cats to examine. They didn't smell too good on their way home. The lady dogs walked home a good few yards up wind from them. Had they been dogs, instead of cats, 'someone' would have suggested a long bath in the *allt*.

There would be more days like this, weather permitting - but weather has always been a problem in Ultima Thule.

taighean dubha - black houses

duileasg – dulse

TOM WARRENER COMES TO THE RESCUE

Vicky, the beautiful Persian cat, and her grown daughter Tigger, were, you remember, the city cats staying with their cousins at *Taigh Glass* at No. 5 Dalmore. Knowing their way around a bit better, they decided to explore the hills above the house on their own - neither Filax nor the dogs Fancy and Jura would be with them. Vicky said that they could move faster, and see more, without the solicitations of Jura their 'guardian', who would always caution them to be careful and not take any risks. "Well", thought Vicky, "how utterly boring life would be if all you cared about was avoiding risk." Jura was a lovely dear, but could be a teeny bit conservative.

They had heard people say that the quickest way to the top of Beinn Dhala Mor was through that long passage called Sgorr Domhnall Duncan, which comprised an enormous split in the rock above *Taigh Glass*. Goodness, they thought, what a dreadful place. It was dark, cold and damp in the passage and everything was covered in wet moss or lichen. It was difficult to maintain ones balance, the floor being so slippery. After a few spills in that hell-hole, they eventually emerged into the fresh air at the top of the Beinn. Tigger resolved never to take that short-cut again, and both wondered why Donald Duncan, the shepherd in times past, had chosen this awful place to say his prayers. Vicky and Tigger jumped from stone to stone to cross the Allt Garbh, which that morning did not live up to its name (fierce river), and climbed further to Beinn Bhrag, the highest point of these hills. The Gaelic *Brag* means 'herd of deer'. Deer? - not for a long time. There is another place in Dalmore with a 'deer name' called *Cnoc na Fheidh*, (hillock of the deer) beside the east side of Loch

Langavat. So, in times past, there were certainly deer here in Dalmore. The view from Beinn Bhrag was magnificent, the more so because our cats were city born and bred. Tigger and her mum rested here for a while, less through tiredness, more in appreciation of the vista before them. From this very spot they could see lochs, rivers, hills, sea cliffs and two beautiful beaches. As they sat there they became aware of a large bird circling high above them, making high pitched cries which left them feeling uneasy. This was no blackbird nor finch which they often hunted around the neat hedgerows back in suburbia. This was a huge bird which came ever closer each time it swept past them. Vicky and Tigger came to the same conclusion and at the same time. Here was a giant raptor which was capable of taking and killing either one or both of them. This was not a raven or a hawk and they decided to move away quietly and hide from this fearful bird. It was only later that Iain Shoudie told them that what they had witnessed was a golden eagle over in the Ghearraidh, where it often builds its huge eyrie. The golden eagle is the largest bird of prey in Britain.

Later, they made their way out the *beinn*, until the big bird dropped out of sight. Here, Tigger decided to climb down from the Beinn and explore the hill opposite, *Cnoc a' Choin*. She did not expect to meet any, but what a strange name for a hill, in the back of beyond! Below the hill on the other side was a slow flowing *allt* and on it what had been a building erected a long time ago. There were two large granite stones still in place, and later she was to learn that this was a corn mill used by the old people of Garenin in times past. Tigger spent some time here on Allt na Muilne, only to realise that she hadn't heard from Vicky for some time now. She retraced her steps to the point on the Beinn where she last saw her mother. Vicky was not there, nor anywhere else along the length of the hill. She did not respond to Tigger's repeated loud cries and this began to worry her a lot. At times like this, it is natural to think of worse case scenarios. Up here on

Beinn Dhala Mor, home to the giant golden eagle, it was easy to conjure up a dreadful outcome. Then there were mink, ferocious and deadly killers, whom some said had escaped from their 'farm'. Our beautiful Victoria was in mortal danger, if not found soon.

Tigger returned to Dalmore at great speed, and raised the alarm. Every cat and dog from every house was mobilised, and search parties organised to cover the whole of that side of the village. Many hours were spent on these searches, but to no avail, and darkness was falling fast. If she was still alive, Vicky would have to spend a cold dark night out on the hill alone. At dawn next morning, as the parties were organising that day's search, Kenny Iceland, the rabbit hunter from the other side of the glen, cleared his throat and asked permission to speak. Jura said that this was a democracy and of course they would all listen to what Coinneach (Kenneth) had to say.

Kenny: "Let's all think now! Who knows the Beinn and the Gearraidh best of all? Who virtually spends all their time there, knows every hillock, every peat bog and of course every rabbit warren?"

Everyone knew to whom Kenny alluded, but that guy wasn't here.

Filax: "Kenny, we all know who you mean, but Navy Tom is a bit of a loner, and can be almost impossible to find in the hills. To be sure, if anyone can locate Vicky, Tom is our man. We would have to find him, before we stood a chance of finding Vicky."

Kenny: "Tom and I are in the same game. We are warreners. Tom does one side of the glen and I do the other. Our hunting techniques are identical and I feel that I could find Tom up there on the Beinn in pretty short time, since time's of the essence."

It didn't take Kenny long to find Big Tom. He emerged from a rabbit hole, his big smiling face covered in sand, looking very much like that *cratur* Bagpuss we hear the children talk about. The hunt was on, Tom in the vanguard and the others at a distance behind, so as not to prejudice Tom's amazing sense of smell. After a little time, on top of Beinn Ia' Ruadh, Tom was seen to freeze where he stood and then made a sort of low strangled call. To the amazement of everyone in the search party, they heard a faint call from a cleft in a rock, close by. It was our Victoria, and she was stuck fast between two rocks, with only her tail protruding. She was in a dreadful state, but still in one piece, as far as Tom could make out.

Tom: "Now, Vicky, the only way we're going to get you out is if I get a grip of your tail in my mouth, and someone takes hold of my tail, and we pull together. What do you think, Old Girl?"

Vicky: "Never mind the 'Old Girl', Tom. Do what you have to, but do it quickly and go easy on that gorgeous Persian tail." Tom had to smile to himself.

Vicky was soon out, and the large group of cats licked our lady clean, well, as clean as a 'cat lick' could. Auntie Dolly gave Vicky a proper bath and dried her at the big peat fire with a warm towel. Hot milk and a lovely piece of haddock followed and our beautiful Persian was then fast asleep.

When Tom, Kenny, and the others, thought of what might have happened they were chastened but comforted to know that Vicky was now safe and sound asleep by the fire. But no one ever again mentioned that Navy Tom had our Vicky by the tail, unless he did so himself!

Cnoc a' Choin – Hill of the Dogs

Eaglais nan Eoin
(The Birds' Church)

I think we would agree that, almost everywhere, there are many more birds than cats and dogs. The West Side of the Island of Lewis is no exception. The religious fervour of the birds in these parts has long been talked of, and many would say that their devotions even exceed those of *Eaglais a' Choin s' Chait*, the Dog and Cat Church in Doune, in charge of which is the Right Reverend MacCollie, the minister who is very attached to his collar. *Eaglais nan Eoin* was situated in the village of Shawbost, which could accommodate large numbers of birds, who flocked to the various Sunday services. They had acquired a large barn of a place in Fibhig, an enormous shed no longer used by the local Harris Tweed mill. Beams and shelving used previously in the mill afforded ideal pews (perches, really) for the large congregations that foregathered there every Sunday. The birds liked their Calvinism dour and unadulterated and this was reflected in a succession of old time avian ministers. Predestination and damnation were favourite themes of these preachers, and favourites too of the congregations. Such were the numbers who came to the Shawbost Church at Fibhig, that multiple meetings of perhaps one thousand birds were required to service this multitude.

The Avian Free Church had the largest congregation on the island, by far. Every bird from the wren to the raven attended these popular services, and all were seated in the

'pews' according to size. There was always a large presence of the crow family (carrion crows, rooks etc.) and, as one would expect, a great variety of seabirds, especially gulls. There were lapwings, sparrows, blackbirds and, up high at the rear of the church, a bevy of buzzards fresh in from the creeks. There was a loft (not an organ loft, mind you) high above the pulpit which was reserved for a particular church member who commanded a lot of respect from others, if not a little fear. This was Gilleasbuig, the golden eagle, who would fly in from Beinn Bhragair to attend these services. Before the Reformation, Gilleasbuig might well have been proud to mention that he was descended from a long line of bishops, but this was something he never spoke of now and, to be sure, neither did anyone else. Gilleasbuig was definitely a presence in the church and he ruffled a few feathers, so to speak, when he flew in to take his pew in the loft. On the few occasions that Gilleasbuig's wife could be persuaded to come (she was not of his persuasion) they said that it was as though the Holy Ghost had passed through the church. The *eoin oig* were always well behaved when Gilleasbuig Mor was in church. His eagle eye could take in the whole congregation without so much as turning his head. The young birds looked straight ahead, wings folded, and not a chirp or a peep from anyone. He was a godsend to the minister and the elders.

The minister of Shawbost Avian Free Church was renowned as a great preacher, and was very often asked to 'guest' at other churches throughout the Hebrides. He was not large of stature but his presence always dominated any company he was in. A carrion crow born in Stornoway, the Reverend Kenneth MacCraw was said to be the 'most powerful' preacher ever heard in the Isles. He was known by all as 'MacCraw Mor', whose powerful message could bring tears to the eyes of the hardest-bitten buzzard. During the communions, a few years back in the Ness Church, it was said that a number of herring gulls had collapsed with the fervour of his preaching, and later became communicants of the church. MacCraw Mor took most of his lessons from the Old Testament, which he felt best reflected the time and travails of his people, much like the Children of Israel long ago. Some people aver that the Celtic peoples are descended from the 'lost tribe of Israel'. The Reverend MacCraw had no doubts about this.

With their souls well nourished, the large congregations would disperse, each bird returning to its own habitat. For Big Gilleasbuig, the golden eagle high up in the loft, an exit strategy had been devised to save the big fella' and the church from damage as he took his leave back to Beinn Bhragair.

In Dalmore, Iain Shoudie was always abreast of matters, and with regards to the events above, his *coilleach*, Calum, and Calum's wife, the *cearc* Fiona, were regulars at the Shawbost Church. Iain Shoudie, as you know, could talk to the animals, and it was he who told me this story. If it were possible, I would loved to have heard MacCraw Mor in full flight, no pun intended.

eoin oig - young birds

Gilleasbuig - Archibald - literally 'the follower of the bishop,

MacCraw Mor - Big MacCrow

coilleach - cockerel

cearc - hen

Heroes of the Airidh (Shieling)

Iain Shoudie rose from the *being* after a refreshing *norrag*. Using the tongs, a relic of the Iron Age, Iain rearranged the glowing embers of the fire, and strategically placed a few peats on top, with the know-how of the seasoned Gael. He managed this despite the presence of various domestic animals around his feet, pets who were settled *ri taobh an theine.* It would be around nine in the evening and soon Murdo (John's brother) would arrive with the two Galloway cows that had grazed all day in the hills over towards Dalbeg. So-Sally, Rupie and Stowlia could hear Murdo opening and closing the gate to the croft up at the back of the house. Oh man! What a sight, as those two majestic black creatures negotiated the doorway to the house, turning left to occupy their own stall in the byre.

With the cows tethered to the wall, Murdo was usually the one who did the milking (a gentle touch, soft comforting words). Those gentle cows would give two large enamel pailfuls of premium milk. There was no skimming, no pasteurising, and for a while no tuberculin testing. There was plenty of milk to go around and Soho (aka So-Sally), Rupie and Stowlia waited around the byre, with the odd meow from the cats. Murdo would assure them that milking was near an end, and in time they all had their bowl or saucer full of that rich warm milk. Murdo and Iain had some supper - bully beef and some 'water waffers' (Jacob's Cream Crackers) and they were all settling to a quiet evening when '*dithis Glass*' arrived from over the way. Fancy, the collie, and his friend, Filax the cat, were made welcome at the warm fireside, just as Iain got the Tilley lamp going. This had the makings of a good *taigh ceilidh* and there was an air of expectation among the animals. Stowlia, the house dog, looked squarely at Murdo, moving his eyebrows up and down, knowing how this rarely failed to take a trick with the boys. *"Murchadh, innis 'inn 'storrie'."* (Stowlia had asked Murdo for a story). Murdo being

the better *seanachaidh* of the two Maclennan men.

Iain Shoudie smiled as Murdo lay his book down on the dresser, and on top he placed his bendy wire 'spegligans'. Murdo adopted a serious demeanour as he returned Stowlia's stare. Stowlia waited a moment before again doing her eyebrows thing. It never failed. A smile began to break over Old Murdo's face, and he was as good as 'hyooked', as Iain would say.

"Am math leat mise a-dheanadh so?"

There was a chorus of barking and meowing, whose meaning was unequivocal. Murdo stirred the peat fire, and its yellow glow lit up the faces of his expectant wee friends. Murdo began his tale of a time past.

Murdo: "You may know, or perhaps not, that our people in the Highlands and Islands, a long time ago, fought for the right to own a few acres of land where they could build a house for their families and grow a few crops. They would no longer fear the heartlessness of the landlords, under whom they were mere serfs. Now they could tend their crofts without interference but there were still a few conditions attached. An important part of the Crofters' Act was the requirement that each summer for a period of six weeks, all animals, mainly cattle, were removed from the crofts to allow the grazings to recover. Crofts of approximately four acres needed a period of regrowth to protect the valuable grasslands. All the cattle were herded onto the adjacent moorland and it is here that generations of people lived out their summers at the *airidhean*, the shielings, so dear to the hearts of successive Lewis families.

The father, grandparents, and some children would remain behind on the croft to look after the crops and perhaps to do some essential repairs about the place. The mother and the rest of her children would travel out to their own *airidh*, basically a small bothy of stones and turf to afford shelter from the rain and the winds, and where they could lay their heads at night. Out there on the *airidh*, the prime concern was the welfare of the cattle, a precious and expensive asset at any time. It would usually fall to the children to tend the cows, moving them to the best pastures and ensuring that they were kept away from other cattle with whom they might fight. This is known as *buachailleachd*, the herding of cattle, and a very important responsibility it was.

"Now, my little friends", said Murdo, "this story will be of particular interest to Fancy and Filax since it involved the Glass family from Gearrannan while at their *airidh* at Tom Liabhrat. The shieling was about a mile south-east of the Dalmore road end, and was located on a small grassy knoll overlooking Loch Tom Liabhrat, a small lochan. Shielings were usually grouped together in small moorland hamlets of people from the same village. Most of the normal activities of the croft were engaged in here, but to a lesser degree. The cooking, baking, milking and washing were carried out in the open, when the weather was fine. There was much to-ing and fro-ing between the croft house in Gearrannan and the *airidh* at Tom Liabhrat. Milk and bread were taken back to the people at home, while peats, flour and other essentials made their way to *Airidh Glass*. At the *airidhean*, lifelong friendships were forged and romantic trysts might one day end in marriage. Children were born at the *airidh*, sometimes people even died there. People went visiting their neighbours to *ceilidh* or perhaps just for a *strupag*. There were banks of blaeberries where the children would sit for hours picking the tiny black berries, sweet and laden with colour. When the sun went down and the oil lamps began to be lit in the *airidhean*, this was truly a wonderful sight, so far out on the lonely moor.

There were many new sights and sounds out here. There were peat workings abandoned long ago with tall towers of turf and heather isolated on the soft floor of peat. For the children of the shielings, this was a magic land inhabited by the *Ni sithiche*. The cry of the corncrake and the lapwing were ever present. There were a few lochs in the area other than Loch Tom Liabhrat around which many of the Gearrannan *airidhean* had been built. Its waters were shallow and it was deemed safe for the children to play in, with so many eyes on them. The little loch provided water for drinking and washing. You couldn't ask for a better site for the shielings.

There were one or two bigger lochs in the vicinity, Feath Loch Gleaharan being no more than half a mile distant. One hot summer afternoon, two young children, Calum Macleod and his sister Catriona, aged four and six respectively, had made their way to Gleaharan and were feeling hot and tired. Against all the warnings that had been given, they decided to cool off in the cold waters of the loch, venturing out until the water was waist high. They were happy cavorting and splashing each other with water. If you only have two legs, these moorland lochs can be very dangerous, what with the cold water, the bottom currents, algae covered stones and all types of plant growth. Nearby, Glass's dog Glen and his pal, Shoudie's Clyde were trying to free some rabbits from their underground homes when they heard a girl's cry for help. Catriona and Calum had lost their footing, but while the little girl

had regained her feet, her brother Calum was being carried out into the loch beyond her reach. Just at that point, Glen and Clyde were by Catriona's side, who pointed frantically towards her brother, now about thirty yards out with his head barely above the water. Glen, who thankfully had all of four legs, plunged into the loch and swam straight for Calum. Holding onto this dear dog's back, Calum was soon safely on the shore with his sister, with whom Clyde had stayed throughout the rescue. Apart from a little spluttering and shivering, the children were safely back in the bosom of their family. Needless to say, our four-legged friends were feted as heroes.

"If this heroic act had taken place now," said Murdo, "then Glen (and possibly Clyde) would have been given the Dickin Medal, the highest award for animal bravery, the equivalent of our Victoria Cross.

"Well, my friends, I hope you enjoyed the story, but it is now bedtime." said Murdo. Actually, Iain Shoudie was already fast asleep up in the room, and one or two of the wee folk were nodding off in front of the fire, beside their pal, Murdo.

ri taobh an theine - at the fireside

'dithis Glass' – the two Glass brothers

seanachaidh - story teller

"Am math leat mise a-dheanadh so?" - Do you want me to do this?

airidh – a hut on the moors (also shieling)

airidhean – plural of airidh

ceilidh – a get-together not always involving music

strupag - drop of tea

Ni sithiche - Little People

Feath - dead calm (Feath Loch Gleaharan)

THE DOGS HAVE THEIR DAY

A blue sky, a few wispy clouds, and it was already warm in Dalmore, this early in the morning. A perfect day for it, but in truth wasn't it a perfect day for just about anything? The Dalmore and Dalbeg fank had happily been arranged for this day. Late July was the time when the sheep and lambs were gathered in from the moors, and the people of the villages always made a day of it. An American lady once stopped to ask what was going on, and why it was called a fank (Gael. *faing*). She dutifully entered the information in her travel diary and spent some time with Seoras perfecting various Gaelic pronunciations. She maintained that a lexicon of Gaelic pronunciations should be included wherever necessary, if the language was to be 'popularised'. Seoras said that Gaelic was still popular enough in Lewis!

Back in Dalmore, preparations were being made for the fank, located in an old gravel pit below Cnoc Na Cartach (Carters' hill) on the main road to Stornoway. Bar a few additions, it was 'ready made' as a fank. Ropes, sacks, shears and dye sticks were gathered, and the women folk prepared some food for the day. The sheepdogs were indispensable in this undertaking for, as ever, where sheep are being worked there you will always find dogs possessed of remarkable skills. Victoria, the blue-cream Persian, asked if cats could be of any help at the fank. Iain Shoudie thanked her kindly but told her that a fank could be a dangerous place for cats and that it is better that they remained within the village, just for today. Jura the black labrador, like Vicky home on holiday from Glasgow, could come along, but purely as a spectator, and must not get involved with the sheep under any circumstances. It might prove very tempting but she must stay well away from the throng of sheep, lambs and sheepdogs. The Shoudie dog, Stowlia, would be at the fank but she was a sheepdog in name only and would be better employed chaperoning Jura for the day. Of the three, Fancy was the only dog of any ability around sheep, but even then was in the second division compared to heavyweights like

Toss, Sweep or Moss. The success of the massive sheep-drive would be down to those three.

Stowlia told Jura that there could be as many as twelve dogs involved and to note how competitive the men were with their dogs. They determined to get a good view of the men and the working dogs as they gathered the sheep from disparate parts of the moor. Beinn na Cloiche (the stony hill), a little way out, stood 525 feet in height and was perfect for the panoramic view it afforded. Stowlia and Jura watched with excitement, tinged with a little envy, as the men gave their dogs the commands that sent them on the long outrun. These were a mixture of Gaelic, English and whistles - "*Mach a' seo*", "Way out" and some more. They had a large area to cover; as far out as Beinn Bhragair, Loch Raoinabhat and Beinn Horshader. The dogs were so far out that they now had to depend on instinct, each working in concert with the others. They would collect stray groups of sheep to add to the drive and, working back and forward, this huge bleating mass was inexorably moving in the direction of the fank, where their masters would take over command for the close quarter work with their dogs. Jura, that gentle dog whose normal daily exercise was a forty five minute stroll in the local woods, was standing on the high vantage point of Beinn na Cloiche, in awe of the scene before her.

Hundreds of sheep and lambs, now driven together, uttered a continuous cry as the more skilled dogs worked back and forward, right and left, helping to shepherd this massive flock through the entrance of the fank. This was a crucial time, when the most determined sheep were wont to break away. Other than Jura and the Shoudies, I wondered who else noticed dear old Stowlia running about at the rear of the other dogs, making out that she too had a contribution to make. She now felt like a real sheepdog, and the wink from Iain Shoudie meant so much to her. Actually, the top dogs like Sweep and Toss could always expect a late foray from Stowlia, but they were happy to oblige her in this yearly flight of fancy.

Talking of Fancy, she had acquitted herself well, according to her peers, and Shonnie, her master, was best pleased with her performance. The fank got under way as the men slowly made their way through this large body of sheep, identifying their own and passing them out to be tied and sheared. Lambs were set aside to be returned to Dalmore. There was much banter and laughter around the fank, and a little beer and whisky was at hand to slake the driest of throats. Some food was taken, sacks bulged with newly shorn wool and the animals were finally released to be driven towards Dalmore, where the sheep and the lambs were parted and the lambs brought inside the village fence. The constant bleating of the lambs and the response of their mothers would fill the valley for days to come. Only the hardest heart could fail to be touched by their cries.

As we now know, cats don't go to fanks, nor do they mix with sheep - not as a rule. But we are aware that there may be 'exceptions to the rule'. Among the lambs which came back to the Shoudie house, was a tiny blackface, which had either been rejected by its mother or the mother had recently died. Iain and Murdo started bottle feeding right away. The cats took this wee lamb to their hearts and in time this small soul started to follow Soho, Rupie and Victoria about the croft. Stowlia the dog could only marvel as the cats gambolled with *'Eobhann an Uan'* (Ewan the Lamb), its name the product of Iain Shoudie's fertile imagination. On cold wet days, Ewan would join Kenny Iceland and the others at the fireside, courtesy of the boys. A lamb warming itself at an open fire - unbelievable, I know, I know.

AWAYDAY ON LOCH ROAG

The weather had been cold and wet these last few days in Dalmore and, strange to relate, it was mid July. I suppose it was no better in Shawbost or Bragair, but today it was calm and the sky was blue. Over at No.4, *Taigh 'Houdie*, Iain had called a meeting of the resident cats and dogs. Soho, Rupie and Guinness were discomfited at the sound of the word 'meeting'. "A meeting," mused Stowlia, "this must be serious. Never heard of a meeting in this house before." Murdo could sense their anxiety and tried to reassure them with a smile.

Iain Shoudie: "Shonnie, over at No.5, wants to discuss a proposition with us, which will also involve the cats and dogs in *Taigh Glass*."

"*O, bhobh*, a meeting - now a proposition. Whatever next?" Stowlia had more than a little of the Jeremiah in her, and was uneasy with what she had heard. The rapid movement of her eyebrows betrayed some anxiety, which in turn unsettled the cats. The meeting was convened outside Shonnie's weaving shed, opposite the hen house.

Shonnie: "We were thinking that, weather permitting, all of you might like a sail in my boat tomorrow afternoon, out on the *caolas* to Loch Roag and the islands off Bernera. It will have to be a very calm day, and we must all behave responsibly while on board. We will have ourselves a picnic on one of the islands, and we may even catch a few fish, for later on."

(In case you are wondering, Shonnie's little address to the animals was simultaneously translated by Iain Shoudie for his little friends).

Any doubts that our wee friends might have harboured were now removed. A general outcry of barks and meowing ensued, partly from relief, but more in excitement at what tomorrow held in store. The cats brushed against Shonnie's and Iain's legs, and Fancy, Stowlia and Jura went barking mad, howling their delight in unison. This, the animals thought, must be the most exciting thing that ever happened to them. Well, to be fair, it isn't often that cats go on a cruise, although dogs have been known to go fishing.

The big day arrived, and the weather was perfect. Well that's what everyone thought - everyone, that is, except Iain Shoudie.

Iain: "If one looks out there on Dalmore Bay, the sea appears calm, from here to the far horizon. A good day to go fishing out of Loch Carloway, you might think. That is not always the case. In this village, by tradition, we were told to examine the state of the waves out there at Rudha na Trileachan, the point out there on the far left of the bay. It could be that the sea looks calm, but if the waves are breaking strongly on the rocks at Rudha na Trileachan, then fair weather cannot be guaranteed out on Loch Roag. But, as you can see, things are fairly calm out there, so the sail is on!

It was by good fortune that Shonnie's cat, Tom, decided to come down from the *beinn* on the very day of the boat trip. You will remember that Tom served on His Majesty's ships during the war (Ratter RNR), before retiring to Dalmore as a warrener. Normally a private individual, Tom was persuaded to join the rest of the 'crew' aboard SY 92, moored at the Dunan at the head of Loch Carloway.

The boat eased itself round the Dunan Pier with Shonnie 'at the helm' and, with the little outboard on full throttle, the boat gently cut its way through the flat-calm of Loch Carloway. They passed the little village of Doune on the port side, and a few minutes later the deserted hamlet of Laimishader appeared on the opposite shore. Shonnie told them that before the pier at the Dunan was built, the remains of an Iron Age fort occupied the site, built nearly 2000 years ago. The beautiful little village of Laimishader had been occupied until about 100 years ago, and had always been known in Lewis as an early Christian site, where miracles could happen. Long after it was a ruin, and up until more recent times, a mother with her sickly child would shelter in the ruins of the church overnight, hoping her prayers would bring healing to her child. Victoria asked Shonnie if sick puppies and kittens were ever taken there by their mothers. Shonnie noted how earnest was Vicky's question, and with a smile, assured her that it was likely - why not?

A gentle breeze passed over the boat, and occasionally one of the crew would have a fine spray of water lick their face. Fancy was properly attired for this sea voyage, wearing, as he was, his full motorcycle gear - leather pilot's jacket, leather flying helmet and a pair of American aviator goggles. She sat beside her master, Shonnie. He gave Fancy a short 'spell at the wheel', but it was difficult, having only *spogs*. Victoria asked Guinness if her blue-cream coat looked OK, what with the wind and the sea spray. "You look smashing, hen", replied Guinness who came from Glasgow. Passing the lighthouse at Aird Laimishader, they were now in the *caolas* proper, where the wind was fresher and the waves a little livelier. Iain Shoudie remarked that the sea was fine, but Jura and Stowlia lay together at the bottom of the boat, feeling a little light-headed.

"We are nearing the island of Little Bernera," said Shonnie, "we will go ashore there to picnic, to look around, and to relax."

The boat slowed as it passed between rocky spurs to reveal the most delightful little golden beach. This little lagoon was home to a number of Atlantic seals, who started barking at the boat's approach. "Do you dogs understand what the seals are saying?" asked Soho. "But of course," answered Stowlia "the Big Fella, there on the rock, is asking if we know his cousin, Ronnie, in Dalbeg Bay." "And do you?" said Soho, with the hint of a Cheshire-like smile on her pretty face.

The boat finally beached on the golden sands of Little Bernera. To be honest, the wee folk were happy to be back on terra firma, and they enjoyed exploring the island with not so much as a house on it. But there once was a farm and house here. In fact, said Iain Shoudie, the first Maclennan to arrive on Lewis was granted the lands of Little Bernera by the overlord of the island, Lord Seaforth, Chief of the Clan Mackenzie.

"And all of the Maclennans on Lewis had their beginnings here, back in around 1700. Murdo and I are descended from that very first Maclennan, the Tacksman of Little Bernera. And before you ask, So-Sally, you are descended from the first Maclennan cat on Little Bernera.

"You will have seen the small graveyard above the beach. That used to be resting place of the Carloway people before the cemetery in Dalmore opened in around 1910. The burial party would have to row all the way out here to bury their loved one. If the weather was stormy, and lasted more than three days, then the body was interred in the little cemetery in Cirbhig, across from the Dunan."

"I could listen all day to Iain Shoudie," said Vicky. "he has a way of making the old times come alive."

Tom Warrener had been fairly quiet throughout the day, and Shonnie noticed it. This would be the first time Tom was at sea, since he served alongside his friend Shonnie in the Royal Navy at the end of the war. Shonnie invited Tom to sit at the stern with him, recalling the time they served together down in England. Shonnie cradled Old Tom in his arms as they turned for home. The men started fishing with the hand-lines and invited the crew to step forward to assist. They struck lucky almost immediately, and within a short time they had enough for a fry-up. Seoras met them at the Dunan with his van and transported skipper, bosun and crew back to Dalmore.

This was a day that they would fondly cherish for years to come. Think about it - cats and dogs fishing for haddock. Quite unbelievable!

O, bhobh - Dear me

caolas – estuary or strait

Rudha na Trileachan - The Oyster Catcher's Headland

Turus ag Iasgaich Anns a Ghearraidh
(A Fishing Trip to the Gearraidh)

It was after lunch, and everyone in the Shoudie house was just coming round after his/her siesta, which in Lewis translates as *norrag* or 'forty winks'. Stowlia, the Shoudie dog, had been sleeping outside on a small knoll of sweet smelling grass, and wakened to see Iain climbing up the outside of the house and onto the *tobhhta*, where he disentangled a long bamboo rod from a covering of rye grass and nettles. The rod was upwards of twenty feet long, thick at one end and tapering to a narrow point at the other. Those bamboos may have come from distant lands, but in the isles they were used for fishing. They were called 'slats' and in Dalmore, no one had to second guess where a man was going with a 'slat'. The best place was over in the Gearraidh, on a rock known as Bandaberie, situated in the wild inlet called Sheilagadh. Bandaberie would normally yield a good catch of fish, but one was always aware of the dangers of fishing there - an exposed rock surrounded on all sides by dangerous swirling eddies.

Stowlia had often gone with Iain to Bandaberie, and she knew how difficult it was to negotiate the descent down a sheer rock face. Fancy and Jura could come along if they wished, as if they would miss out on such an adventure. They would have to wrap up against the cold winds, as they could be out on Bandaberie for some time. Stowlia was endowed with a thick coat of hair, but Fancy and Jura were not so well padded. Fancy had her pilot's outfit, of course, but Jura, the labrador, with its smooth black coat, would need some extra cover. Aunt Dolly came up with the ingenious idea of adapting an old Harris guernsey (minus sleeves) as a body warmer for Jura. It was a coat of many colours, knitted from a mixed-bag of bobbins.

They crossed high above the beach, 'outside the fence', heading for Geodha na Muilne and the Gearraidh. Here, on these green slopes which were known as *Nan Eilidean*, they encountered Tom Warrener emerging from a rabbit burrow, covered in sand from the top of his head to the tip of his tail. They exchanged a few pleasantries with Tom, but they could see that he was eager to return to the work in hand. The fishing party eventually reached Bandaberie, and although there was a bit of a swell on the sea, it was decided that fishing was possible but only if a lot of care was taken. Generations of the women folk of Dalmore feared for the men who fished on Bandaberie. Iain Shoudie decided that it was better and safer for Stowlia and Co. to stay up top, and to watch the operations from a clear vantage point, 25 feet up the sheer rock face. The waves hitting the rocks were moderately strong, but the plinth on which Iain stood was as yet safe. Ground bait of cold boiled potato tossed into the ravine had spectacular effects as Stowlia, Fancy and Jura witnessed Iain's bamboo bending time after time, the line alive with wriggling fish. Of course, Jura had never witnessed anything like this (understandably so), but her excited barking drew smiles from her country cousins. This was something to tell Solas and Fred back in Glasgow. With his bag full, Iain stopped fishing and carefully scaled the rock face. "Well, my friends, we'll have a great fry-up tonight, along with Murdo and the cats," said John.

"Since Jura has come all the way from Labrador," said 'An 'Houdie, "we must show her round this little bit of Lewis." Jura appreciated Iain's stab at metaphor! "Firstly, I must find a place to leave the fish, as it's quite a heavy load to carry." He deposited the hessian bag of fish behind a large rock, well out on Rudha an Trileachan, where man never ventures. The attention of the three dogs was drawn to the large amount of sea shells strewn across the ground here. It was like a 'midden', a word known to both archaeologists and Glaswegians alike. This was the drop zone where sea birds would release their newly caught shell fish from on high, smashing them on the rocks below. Moving downhill a little, Fancy was first to reach Allt na Muilne where in past times the people would grind their corn or oats in one of the two corn mills located on the steeply descending river (Allt na Muilne - The stream of the mills). Fancy and her two friends explored inside the old stone walls of the mills, splashing about in the semi-darkness. The cool waters of the *allt* was a footbath like none other.

Over at Sheilagadh, a broad deep inlet with a rocky beach, they could see from the powerful wave movements that this was a dangerous place, on whose shore all sorts of flotsam and jetsam were strewn - reminders of the position that Lewis occupies at a crossroads of the Atlantic's waterways. Sheilagadh is an ugly, unforgiving place. They rejoined the *allt* further up its course, where now it is called Allt a' Ghearraidh. There were some small trout in the river, and Stowlia tried her hand (*spogs* actually!) at *guddling*, much to the amusement of her companions. Result? A wet dog, no poissons.

At this moment, they espied three horses emerge from behind Cnoc a' Choin. Jura asked if Stowlia or Fancy knew any of these dogs. Iain Shoudie laughed and awaited their reply. "Jura, that was a long time ago," replied Fancy "but I think my grandmother may have known one of them." Charlie, Jimmy and Tom were Dalmore's three horses, who were free to roam the common grazings unless they were needed for work on the croft - ploughing, carting peats and hay etc. Charlie was Shonnie Glass's horse, a chestnut stallion, a tireless worker with an excellent temperament. But he also valued his freedom, and played hard to get when summoned for work. Shonnie would send his nephew, Iain, up into the hills, to find the horses and bring Charlie back to the croft for a spot of work. Charlie often shares this story with Jimmy and Tom.

"You can see wee Iain approaching from afar calling my name - very touching, really. Bare-footed, he wears a pair of long short trousers, a tweed jumper (of course) and his hair is cut in the mandatory pudding-bowl style. He carries a bridle and bit in one hand, and half a Stornoway loaf in the other. Tearing the bread in two, he approaches nearer, calling me, and proffers the bread. Just as I take the bread, he tries to get the bit into my mouth and the bridle over my ears. Jerking my head to the side, I gallop off to join you two. Now, I know that should he fail again, the lad would have a long trek home for more bread, with no guarantee of success the next time. So, a while ago I resolved to allow my capture on the second offer of bread. I shake my head, neighing loudly, but I open my mouth to accept the bit, and my surrender is complete. For Iain, the wee Glasgow boy, there is great pride in this achievement. For me, it's a harmless piece of fun, and I'm only too happy to oblige the wee fella'."

"Time to head back home", said 'An 'Houdie as they made their way across the old *lazybeds* in the Gearraidh. Climbing up towards Rudha an Trileachan, they could hear the hellish shrill cries 'of a thousand birds'. There, in front of them, huge gulls were engaged in a battle royal over the contents of Iain's bag of fish, hard won at Bandaberie. The seagulls dispersed, leaving a sorry mess of fish strewn across the grass but, on closer examination, about half the catch was untouched and would be on the frying pan later. A grand banquet and soiree was planned for the old *taigh dubh* that night.

Tobhta - In the traditional Lewis thatched house (1830-1900), sometimes called a *taigh dubh* (black house), there were double walls, and in between a turf infill. The walls were about 6 feet thick and rose to a similar height. The timbers which supported the thatch originated at the inside edge of the inner wall. When complete, there was a turfed 'path' all the way round the *taigh dubh*. This was the *tobhta*.

Guddling (a Scots word) involves fishing for trout/salmon in a river, by gently placing your hands under the fish and tickling its underside. When the fish is in rapture, you sweep the fish up, and onto the river bank. Poachers sometimes guddled a salmon – 'one for the pot'.

Lazybeds - In early days, with only a spade or *croman* (hoe) for digging, parallel ditches were excavated to afford ground drainage, and the soil was heaped up on top between ditches to give ground for growing some crops. Lazy? I think not.

Nan eilidean - Fallow grounds. Here the short grassy ground fell away steeply to the sea.

THE CARLOWAY AGRICULTURAL SHOW
OTHERWISE KNOWN AS THE CATTLE SHOW

The biggest event in the District of Carloway was the Annual Agricultural Show, held each summer on the first Wednesday in August. Better known locally as the 'Cattle Show', it drew large crowds of people from all over the Island of Lewis, and competitors from Shawbost to Garynahine (indeed, 'all points West'). It was the longest surviving show on the island (since 1911), known affectionately as 'Lewis's Premier Show'. By dint of sheer numbers, it could easily have been called 'The Sheep Show'. The title 'Agricultural Show' was possibly to appease those in the Board of Agriculture or the Crofters Commission who were keen to see crofting adopting more modern agricultural methods, but obviously on a smaller scale, by introducing better breeding programmes in cattle and sheep, mechanising hay making for winter feeding and reclaiming the moorland using fertilisers, sand, and surface seeding. Still, it has always been known as the Cattle Show.

The weather was fair when the big day came around, (old memories, fine weather?) and many animals would be transported to Carloway to compete for prizes at the show. Dalmore's 'Famous Five', Soho, Rupie and Stowlia from *Taigh 'Houdie* and Fancy and Filax from *Taigh Glass* were going along for the first time, as were their city cousins, Jura, Victoria and Guinness. I know - they were domestic animals but the show committee had decided in their wisdom to include, this time round, competitions for Best Dog in Show and for Best Cat.

Victoria, the blue-cream Persian' was entered in the Cat Show
under her pedigree name of Victoria Chantelle Lautrec and,
as they say, she was definitely 'up for it'. Jura, the Black
Labrador Retriever, was not so keen but Fancy said that it
would be a 'hoot', or something 'cheery' like that in Gaelic.
The main competition animals - cattle, sheep, horses and
poultry - were either walked down to the showground at
Carloway or ferried there by tractor and trailer. Donald John
would be in charge of Daisy, Shonnie's beautiful brown
Ayrshire milk cow, and Donald, his older brother, would
accompany Morag, the young heifer, the finest specimen of
Shorthorn you would ever see this side of Stornoway. She had
already been sold to Angus Macdonald, well known
auctioneer and butcher from town, for a princely sum.

Daisy and Morag and their two *buachaille* left early to walk to
Carloway. Jimmy, the horse, didn't have the necessary
'hands' to compete. He wasn't bothered. Everyone in the
district took pride in their sheep and, consequently, entries in
all sheep categories were high. Shonnie was entering some
wedders, lambs and a powerful looking Blackface ram. They
would go down by tractor, in some cages improvised for the
purpose. Getting them onto the trailer had been difficult,
until Guinness the Gall suggested that digestive biscuits were
regularly employed as bait by the shepherds on the hill farms
of the mainland. And it worked! They mounted the trailer and
entered the cages, just like sheep, as the saying goes.
Shonnie gave Guinness a gentle clap, in way of thanks, and
Guinny-Goo was happy to advance farming know how in this
crofting community.

'Balaich Shoudie' went along with Stowlia, Soho and Rupie,
their 'domestics'. Kenny Iceland, the 'cat who comes in from
the cold' (occasionally) was capable of making up his own
mind whether to go to the show. *'An 'Houdie* would leave him
a 'Dolittle' note, but it was unlikely that Kenny would come.
Like Garbo, he wanted to be alone. The Shoudie Boys made

quite a show as they emerged from the *taigh dubh* wearing their special visiting clothes - newish cap, black polished shoes etc. Iain wore his 'Chicago' hat, with the brim pulled down over one eye, just like that fellow Dillinger in America. There would be many old friends at the Carloway Show and Murdo and Iain knew that the *comhradh* flowed more easily with a few drams of whisky; it also made them better judges of the cattle and sheep paraded in the ring, they believed!

The show wasn't just about animals. Experts were at hand to judge knitwear, articles fashioned in wood or metal, woven Harris Tweed, vegetables grown on the croft, scones and cakes baked in the croft house and a variety of other categories. There was an open piping competition with entries from Callanish to Canada and from New Shawbost to New Brunswick. Highland games were in most cases trials of strength as was the final event of the day, the inter village boat race involving perhaps a dozen boats down on Loch Carloway, by the Dunan. In fact, the last event of the day (by rights it was night) was the Cattle Show Dance in the Drill Hall which started around midnight when none of the Dalmore crew would be present.

Usually a noted personage was invited to open the show, a person who had advanced his standing during his lifetime, people like lawyers, scholars, journalists and even teachers, of which there was no shortage. Even a peer of the realm deemed such an invitation a great honour. This year, for some reasons, the 'Comm-it-tee' had failed to engage a *duine mor* to perform the opening ceremony. Why? No one could, or would, say! Fancy, however, heard from some of the Garenin dogs that a last-minute replacement had been found, an Aberdonian of no particular note, whose instant acceptance amazed some members of the committee leaving them no time to reconsider their invitation, if that was their wish. Word of this spread quickly among the animals at the show. It would be a little later before the people learned that a Mr.

Grant would open the Carloway Agricultural Show. His name was understandably absent from the show programme, a name which otherwise would have meant little to the people of the district, bar a few to whom it meant something else again. A tall, heavy set man, Grant projected a faux bonhommie, and a barely disguised bombast. He had been involved in a variety of businesses, but never for too long. He would never risk his own money on any business venture, preferring to invest in other people's. There was not a grant nor subsidy which he didn't know about and for those who asked he was generous with advice, since this increased his standing but at no cost to himself. His reputation grew among those who were like-minded. His meanness was a study in pathology, but this was not easily discerned as it was masked by his largesse, using multiple expense accounts. He would often tell people that he was a millionaire, which he probably was. No matter where, he would regale perfect strangers with stories of his business acumen and his wealth. "I'm a millionaire, you know." This became his mantra. He would shortly open the show.

"Fancy, who told you so much about Mr. Grant?", asked Filax. "It was one of the Garenin dogs, whose master got useful advice from Grant about a sheep subsidy" replied Fancy.

Mr. Grant's cri de coeur was "I love Carloway", a bit like the sycophants who extol their love of America, yet he was only in Carloway for two weeks a year. He was jocular, in a 'hail fellow, well met' sort of way, possessed of a host of jokes, which he had honed over the years. He did not allude directly to his millionaire status, but the crowd were left in no doubt that here was a man of import. Finally, the Show was declared Open. Stowlia was awakened by the ripple of applause around her.

There was much to see at the show, and Iain 'Houdie would be guide and interpreter to the Dalmore animals for the rest of the afternoon, unless Iain was called away on an urgent matter of state which could be settled, he said, with a small libation. Over at the sheep pens, the judging was taking place. Large men of rosy complexion, tweed jacket and plus-fours, were pulling and prodding the sheep, examining their teeth, and engaging in other technical procedures, unknown to anyone other than the big man in the fore-and-aft hat, who was probably your head man (no pun intended). Shonnie's sheep lost out to some beautiful specimens from Breasclete and Garenin but they would not return to Dalmore in the trailer disgraced, by any means. Anyway, there was a whole packet of digestive biscuits to ease the pain! Stowlia, Fancy and Jura were keen to help them on board! In the cattle ring, however, Shonnie was doubly successful with first prizes (and money) for our lovely Ayrshire cow, Daisy, and that superb specimen, Morag the heifer. Some moments to savour!

Horses measured in hands (why - asked Jura?) and hens and cockerels all came under the scrutiny of an appropriate expert. The large blousey lady handling the poultry was known to all as *Cailleach a' Chearc.* Sloppy pronunciation could lead to the lady being called *Coileach a' Chearc* and that would not do.

The Dog and the Cat Shows were not like Crufts etc. but were only small local 'beauty contests', not to be taken too seriously. Jura, the smooth coated Labrador Retriever, pipped Toss Macarthur for top dog but, to be honest, this wasn't Jura's thing at all. Now, the Cat contest was very much Victoria's thing. As a pedigree Persian, with a fabulous blue-cream coat and blazing orange eyes, she was the feline equivalent of Zsa Zsa Gabor. This was a more bitchy, back-biting affair than the Dog Show, and after much scratching and caterwauling, Victoria Chantelle Lautrec was declared the winner. Away at the back of the crowd, the unmistakable head of Kenny Iceland appeared, with the hint of a smile. A few eyes popped as Vicky moved towards the judge to receive the red rosette for first prize. Her studied walk, with her bushy tail prescribing a figure of eight, might be thought of as 'sexy', but I'm sure that was not her intention. The male moggies at the front of the cat walk were too excited to care. However, the result did not suit the small cat-coterie from Garynahine. "That cat is a ringer, Sylvia. I'm sure I saw the bugger at the Tolsta Show". The old *bodach* from Shawbost could not get his head around the idea of blue cream. "They must be getting a subsidy for that. I wonder if Bodach Grant knows anything about this?".

The traditional island games of tossing the sheaf, putting the stone and lifting the weights was dominated by the success in all of them of young Alex Beag from Heather Street - this was a great feat considering the strength of his opponents. Tossing the caber is never a feature of Lewis games because there are no trees on the island, The inter-village tug-of-war resulted in victory for the men of Upper Carloway. The final event of the Show was the boat race down on Loch Carloway to which the entire show crowd repaired. This was no Henley Regatta, but an event requiring strength and tactics. They were rowing for their village and reputations were at stake. These were large wooden, clinker boats requiring six oars to propel the vessel a measured distance down a sea loch. The oarsmen were Lewis bred and many of them would have had sea-going experience. As the boats surged through the waters, it was easy to transport your mind to a time when the *birlinns* of the Macdonalds, Lords of the Isles, could be seen coming up Loch Carloway, oars moving as one and banners stiff in the breeze.

"What a day, what a day", said Iain 'Houdie, which Soho thought might have been slightly slurred. "And why not", she mused, "*air latha a' Chattle Show* ".

I nearly forgot. The men from Doune won the boat race.

buachaille – herdsmen

comhradh – conversation

duine mor - an important man or man of consequence

Cailleach a' Chearc - the Old Hen Lady

Coileach a' Chearc – the Old Hen cockerel!

bodach – old man

birlinns – Scottish boats often used around the Hebrides

"air latha a' Chattle Show" - on the day of the Cattle Show

THA DITHIS CAIT A POSAIDH AN A SIABOST
(TWO CATS ARE TO MARRY IN SHAWBOST)

"Two cats are to marry in the village of Shawbost". This was the headline in the Stornoway Gazette and if Donnie Large had not written the article, people would have taken this as some sort of April Fool, even in mid July. "Could this be true?" people asked, "And if it is, God help us all. Can you imagine what the Daily Express will make of this?"

"Well," said Catriona Bheag, "the Express features the adventures of a walking, talking bear called Rupert, who wears a *guernsey dearg agus briogais buidhe* and yet everyone I know thinks nothing of it. Two of his friends are Bill Badger and Edward Trunk; so if you can believe in a bear who lives in a cottage with his mother and father, and travels to fantastic places around the world with a badger and an elephant, then why are you so surprised at two young Lewis cats getting married?". Everyone agreed loudly with Catriona (they usually did) and wished the couple a happy life together.

Of course, every cat (dog and bird too) on the West Side knew of the forthcoming wedding between Eilidh (Helen) and Uisdean (Hugh), two of the nicest cats one could ever know. Many of them had attended the *reitich* the previous year in Shawbost and that was a night to remember. "*O, a' Bhalaich*", said Donnachadh Bronach, "Poor Uisdean will need all of his nine lives from now on." With the withering look on Catriona Bheag's face, Duncan was quick to point out that it was joke ("A joke, Kate, a joke, for goodness sake!") Kate smiled. "You seemed to have forgotten, Duncan, that Helen too has nine

79

lives and, I'd wager, a few more besides." Those from the mainland might have been surprised that the *Leodhaisaich* and the Lewis born animals were so good *aig A' bheurla* (at speaking English). People in Shawbost were nowadays very much at ease with English. The bilingual programme had been a great success in this district. A facility with English, and particularly as it related to the finer points of bureaucracy, was well established and thoroughly rehearsed in the popular evening classes. Photocopies of blank forms relating to grants and subsidies were issued repeatedly and the class required to fill in the appropriate answers in English, until all were word perfect. Carloway had mastered the niceties of 'the English' a long time ago.

The day of the wedding had arrived and the 'Dalmore Crew', all of whom had been invited, were getting themselves washed and spruced up over at *Taigh Glass*, with Dolly and Shonnie in attendance. Washing, drying, brushing and combing were the order of the day. Victoria, our recently crowned beauty queen, was carefully brushed and her 'fur coat' sprinkled with Lily of the Valley talcum powder. A little pink bow was attached on top of her head, between her ears. She looked a picture! The three lady dogs were thoroughly washed down at the *allt*. After a good shake, and a dry-out in the wind and sun, Stowlia, Fancy and Jura went up to the house where Dolly gently brushed their coats. There was a sheen on Soho's beautifully black coat, like a panther in miniature. Guinness and Rupie were attended to and were now eager to make their way to Shawbost. Down from the hills came Kenny Iceland and Tom Warrener, our two rabbit hunters, who normally shied away from crowds but who now craved the company of their own kind. They had come 'down from the creeks', and were happy to make the acquaintance of some old friends. Seoras (George Macleod) had offered to transport them all to the wedding in his dinky little Austin van.

They were singing *puirt a' beul* on the way to Shawbost. Tom Warrener was up on his hind legs doing a hornpipe, holding his front *spogs* high enough in the air to touch the roof of the van. What happy times this brought to mind, the times he danced on the mess table to entertain the sailors during the war. Kenny Iceland wondered what had possessed his pal, Tom. Perhaps he had descended from the hills too quickly – 'the bends' so to speak. As they approached Shawbost, there were white flags to be seen all along the sides of the road. The crowds of animals were growing apace. They were, in the main, cats and dogs but there were some sheep and lambs and a fair number of birds. Mrs Tunnag from Dalmore was quacking loudly, and presumably happily, as she waddled down the road past Loch Grinabhat with her ducklings in tow. While Helen and Hugh's wedding did not quite have the caché of a Burton-Taylor extravaganza, there is no doubt that it would be the largest *latha posadh* ever seen on Lewis. To say that this wedding was unique in the annals of the animal world did not quite do justice to this marvellous event. But the national press and television companies knew that this was a story that would run and run. The Stornoway hotels were full. Journalists like Mary Marquis, Magnus Magnusson and Ludovic Kennedy were transported to Stornoway to cover the big show in Shawbost. David Attenborough was there to interview the young feline newlyweds, from the mammalian perspective of course. They were to be married in the Avian Free Church at Fibhig in Shawbost, because it was a huge building and because it was the only animal church in Helen's village. The Dog and Cat Church was too far away in Doune. The service was to be conducted jointly by the Reverend MacCraw of the Shawbost Free and The Right Reverend MacCollie of the Established Church in Doune.

The crow family were gathering in numbers, as were many species of sea birds. Dogs and cats of every description and from every place were heading for the Shawbost Avian

Church. The wee birds, like the wrens and sparrows, had flown in early for front row seats. Gilleasbuig Mor, the golden eagle from Beinn Bhragair appeared, out of the blue so to speak, with his wife and her brother, the Kaiser from Harris. O' man! What a sight that was, as they appeared out the mist like three massive Vulcan bombers. The Dalmore group were by now very excited as they entered the church. There was a capacity congregation, and anybody who arrived now would need to take a pew outside on the *creagan*. The ushers at the church were a group of very cool rooks, in their shiny black attire, collectively known as the 'Blues Brothers' and inside, on either side of the pulpit, sat a dozen carrion crow, elders of the Shawbost Avian Free Church. You could not say that these lads were 'cool'. There would be no organ nor hymns, only the Psalms of David, precented by that Nightingale from Ness, Kate Mhor, sister of the bride.

Eilidh and Uisdean made a fine couple as they took their vows in front of the two reverend gentlemen, and as they walked out the church as a married couple of cats, a ripple of applause spread through the church, which actually brought a smile to the faces of the two ministers - in a Free Church, mind you!

Press and television were there in numbers but Donnie Large was the first to interview Eilidh and Uisdean for the 'Cassette'. They were all there, the BBC in Stornoway with Neen Mackay, BBC Scotland with Mary Marquis and Ludo Kennedy for the Tonight programme in London. The *Sasunnaich* found this story hard to swallow - imagine! Iain Shoudie did well as interpreter for the animals, who were constantly interviewed by the media scrum. Doing his 'Dolittle' job, Iain was making a 'packet' of money – "*torr airgead, a' bhalaich, torr airgead*". He spent some of it (most, actually) with his brother, Murdo, down at Doune in the company of Fyfe Robertson and Ludovic Kennedy. Iain did enjoy this kind of attention.

The wedding dinner was al fresco (a new departure) and to accommodate the vast number of guests, multiple sittings were required, right into the night. Helen and Hugh attended each sitting, seated at either end of a long white sheet. People came forward and placed their gifts in front of Helen. Of course, the married couple did not eat at all the sittings. The food was excellent and the entertainment and dance would be remembered for a long time to come. Everything prepared for that day and everyone who attended, were testament to the love the people had for Eilidh and Uisdean

Our little friends from Dalmore arrived back home in the early hours, exhausted but elated. The electric light (the only one in the house) was still on in *Taigh Shoudie* and from the music and laughter, one might think that the wedding *ceilidh* had shifted from Fibhig over the *beinn* to Dalmore.

No one could say when this *ceilidh* would end!

> *guernsey dearg agus briogais buidhe* - red jumper and yellow trousers
>
> *O, a' bhalaich* - O, boy!
>
> *Leodhaisaich* - Lewis people
>
> *puirt a' beul* - mouth music; *latha posadh* - wedding day
>
> *creagan* – hillock; *Sasunnaich* - English people
>
> *torr airgead, a' bhalaich* - lots of money, boy

FRED AND THE EAGLES

When the '*Fear Dubh*' was around, and he had been around for some time now, no young animal, bird or fowl was safe from him. His territory stretched from New Shawbost in the north through Dalbeg and Dalmore, to Upper Carloway and Garenin in the south. The 'Black One' in question, was a large black male mink, a long-term escapee, and these were his 'killing fields'. He was the sole ground predator in the area, and didn't always kill for food. Killing was often sport for the mink. Normally the mink will kill and eat fish from the river, nesting birds and their chicks, and very often hens, cooped up in the hen house. It is in this latter situation that you see the mink at its deadliest and most ruthless.

Within a few minutes the mink will dispatch up to twenty hens in a gratuitous orgy of killing. It will feed only on the viscera of perhaps three birds, eschewing totally the flesh. In such circumstances, the large part of his kill is 'for sport'. In a short time he might be a long way off, indulging his sport in some other killing field. With an ongoing supply of food, the mink can range far and wide and is almost impossible to locate, never mind eliminate. For the most part it travels unseen, and often strikes under the cover of darkness. The bloody carnage it leaves in its train is unmistakably the mark of the mink. So, people and animals in Dalmore were alert to the dangers posed by this escaped mink and took whatever measures they could to trap or kill the 'Black One'. This could be very difficult, and even fatal for a small animal to attempt.

One morning, a week into the alert, So-Sally and Rupie took a walk down to the *traigh* for nothing more than a stroll along the golden strand, caressed by the waves of the Atlantic and overlooked by the oldest rocks on earth. On the way back past the *allt*, they noticed that Mrs Tunnag and her family of ducklings were not swimming in the river, as was their wont. Climbing down the sandy *bruach*, they followed the river's course well into Lot a' Bhoer (the Boer's croft) and it was only after a thorough search, that they discovered Mother Duck and her off-spring hiding under a bank of peat well away from the river. Soho approached the ducks and could see that Mrs Tunnag was in a distressed state. Her ducklings were hidden from view beneath her. Her beautiful black beak was streaked with tears, and her voice was just a whimper. She told how the previous day she was leading her little ducklings along the river bank, when out of nowhere, and in an flash, a large mink attacked and killed two of her offspring. She asked that Soho and Rupie search along the river and bury her beautiful *tunnagean* by the *allt* where they were reared. The Shoudie cats tried as best they could to comfort Mrs Tunnag and her three remaining ducklings but, in any case, they led them to the safety of the barn at *Taigh a' Bhoer*.

The animals in Dalmore and Dalbeg convened a parliament the following morning, on the *creagan* behind *Taigh Glass* to discuss all matters relating to the '*Fear Dubh*', the black mink which in a short time had brought fear and death to the *Dailean*. People might lose a few hens which would cost them some money but, for the animals, this was something else altogether, a seriously frightening situation which would not be easily resolved.

Stowlia: "I spoke to '*An 'Houdie* about this grave situation and asked him to alert Shonnie, Murchadh a' Bhoer and Iain Beag na Cnamhan, the three men in the village with shotguns, but the real problem is locating the mink before a shot is fired."

Rupie: "I can't see any of us cats, even So-Sally, being a match for an adult male mink. This one, the *Fear Dubh*, is a particularly 'bad stick'. We will of course do all in our power to help, but I fear that it falls to the dogs to take the major role in this business."

Jura: "Such fine prose, Rupie. I can see the influence of James Shaw-Grant in the Stornoway Gazette. The Sunday Times of London rated the "Cassette" very highly indeed."

Fancy: "Shonnie has a wee white ferret with red eyes, which he uses to catch rabbits, but it would be useless against this natural born killer. I fear that we must devise a master plan to trap and kill our foe, and one which minimises the risk to us all. There is no time to waste, so thinking caps on, everyone."

Victoria: "As experienced and as tough as Tom Warrener and Kenny Iceland are, our hillbilly friends are still cats, and this mink is bigger, faster and extremely vicious. However, they could play an important part in our plan, if and when we devise one. Fancy is right in saying that we have no time to waste. We owe it to those ducklings and hens, to rid our villages of this unnatural predator. He's an American, for goodness sake!"

It began to sound like the deliberations of The Famous Five on one of their picnics, with lashings of ginger beer.

Jura: "The land cover in the village is a mix of heather, short grass, *machair* land and *feannags* of corn or potatoes. He must be flushed out from hiding into the open ground. If we can't see the mink, we have no way of trapping him. But, help might yet be on its way. I had earlier asked Shonnie if we could invite my wee friend, Fred, from Renfrew up for a couple of weeks and Shonnie said 'Yes, if Fred can make do in the weaving shed.' "

Stowlia: "Pardon me, but who is this Fred, and how can he help us?"

Jura: "Fred is a 'Parson Russell Terrier'. Basically, he is a Jack Russell Terrier with longer legs and, in his case, a rough coat of white, black and tan. He has, as they say, 'a nose like God knows'. He is very swift, can turn on the space of a sixpence and is both fearless and tenacious. The Reverend John Russell crossed his terrier with a fox terrier to get a dog with longer legs who could keep up with the hunt and of course flush out the fox from its bolt hole. I am hoping he can do the same for us with the *Fear Dubh*."

Fancy: "For aerial reconnaissance, we have enlisted the help of our friends, the golden eagles. Gilleasbuig and his brother-in-law, the Kaiser from Harris are delighted to be part of our mink hunt. Gilleasbuig has asked that the gunmen refrain from shooting at them, as they usually do when the eagles fly high across Dalmore. They are now here to help, not harm."

The next morning, Fred the Terrier was introduced to the rest of the hunting party and, nodding in the direction of the eagles, he whispered very quietly to Jura 'Big Man, who the hell are they?' Although Fred was a dog with attitude, he and the eagles seemed to bond in no time (a little time, perhaps). This really had to be seen to be believed. Iain Shoudie and Murdo rehearsed them thoroughly in what would be required in the hunt for the Black One. Fred and the eagles would have the leading roles, while everyone else would act as beaters but only when directed to by Jura, overall coordinator of manoeuvres. The eagles and Fred rehearsed call signs that would be used. The shrill cry of the birds and Fred's piercing bark announced the start of the hunt. Yet they realised that they could not underestimate the guile and intelligence of their deadly foe.

Kenny Iceland and some of the 'beaters' kept to the northern parts of the village and hill, familiar to Kenny. He and his party would move in a line, raising hell by barks and mewing, in order to force the Black One towards the *machair* where the grass was short. Kenny would inspect any rabbit burrows or overhangs as the hunt progressed. Tom Warrener and party covered the other half of the village. Jura, hunt coordinator, and Fred occupied the centre ground, at all times ready for action. Gilleasbuig and the Kaiser were 'the eyes in the sky', as they say, taking long slow sweeps across the glen. With these lads flying high, shotguns were now redundant for which the boys from Beinn Bhragair were thankful. Having done one sweep of the valley, it was repeated by broadening the net.

There was no result on Day One, but towards the end of the second day, the eagles spotted the undulating movement of a black animal at Geodha an Uillt, near the cliffs on the north side of Dalmore Bay. Jura barked her orders that everyone, except Fred and the eagles, were to fall back. Fred was soon in place by the cliffs, waiting for instructions from Gilleasbuig who, with the Kaiser, was circling on high. At the word, Fred nosed his way from one rabbit hole to another, partly entering each and giving a muffled bark. There was an explosion of action now as the *Fear Dubh* emerged from a burrow. Fred moved quickly and carefully towards the mink, who turned menacingly towards him. As Fred halted, he heard and felt this phenomenal rush of air behind him to see Gilleasbuig carry off the Black One in his mighty talons to a high *creag*, a little way off. The eagles were left with their prey, and the animals could live their idyll of life in the *Dailean*. Mrs Tunnag resumed her life on the *allt* with her ducklings; the eagles went back to Beinn Bhragair and Iain Shoudie sat on the bench outside the *taigh dubh*, smoking his Golden Virginia and holding his animal audience in thrall with tales of derring-do, 'always new, and always true'. Stowlia just smiled.

Fear dubh – The Black Man

allt - river

bruach - steep bank

tunnagean - ducklings

taigh a' Bhoer - the Boer's house

Iain Beag na Cnamhan - Wee Iain 'Bones'

machair - shoreline grass land

feannags - strip fields

Geodha an Uillt - the cove or creek of the burn

creag - rock

Dailean - the Dales (Dalmore and Dalbeg)

THE TRAVELLERS MAKE CAMP IN DALMORE

In Lewis, as in other islands of the Hebrides, there was little in the way of motorised transport to be seen on the single track roads, except for vehicles with a very specific purpose. In the early 1950s, each district could boast of having a few buses and lorries, usually owned and run by an established family of entrepreneurs who probably also had the local shop. There was a small number of vans which 'brought the town to the village' - essential groceries, clothes (Co-op Drapery), post office van, mobile library, travelling bank, fish van (herring mostly) and of course the Harris Tweed lorries, keeping the weavers supplied and returning to the mill with the finished tweeds. To get about the district, you hoofed it or, as was becoming increasingly popular at this time, you bought yourself a sturdy bicycle, a Raleigh or a Rudge. There was perhaps the odd motorbike, but saloon cars were frankly rare, the local doctor's being such a rarity. The ministrations of midwife and nurse were usually accompanied by bicycle (doctor's car in emergencies). Non-urgent religious matters could normally be dealt with by the minister on the Sabbath. In Dalmore, with its cemetery-by-the-sea, we often had occasion to see a long black carriage passing slowly through the village. Glass-sided to reveal a fine oak coffin, this was a hearse on hire from the Stornoway undertakers, which transported the deceased to their final resting place by the *traigh*. In many respects, you could say that this was a van, albeit a very special van, which no one stopped because it had nothing to sell. Now, a different vehicle had arrived in the village, and it had not come alone.

This morning, Rupie was the first to emerge from *Taigh 'Houdie*. Murchadh had just got the fire going and there was a good deal of bluish smoke rising from the stone chimney, snaking its way up the *beinn* at the back of the house. Rupie went through the elaborate cat ritual of cleaning herself with her tongue and the deft use of her white *spogs*. Looking around her, Rupie's eyes happened on a strange scene at the corner of the cemetery nearest the *allt*. There were two round tent like dwellings, with wisps of smoke coming from the top

of one and a small lorry parked at the side of the tents. There was the sound of children's laughter and the barking of dogs. At that moment, Iain Shoudie, cup of tea in hand, came out to sit on the bench and immediately lit a Senior Service. So-Sally sat close to Iain on the bench, which amounted to a long heavy plank supported at each end by some breeze blocks. At the end nearest the door, there were two white enamel pails used to hold water from the old spring well situated below a large rock at the base of the *beinn*. Very cold and pure, this water had the reputation of being the best in the village.

Iain Shoudie*: "A' Ghille, thoir suil air sinn.* It's good to see them back in Dalmore. It's a few years since they made camp here."

Rupie: "I don't remember seeing them here or anywhere else but Soho, being that bit older than me, may well know who they are. There was a hint of a smile on Rupie's face as she turned towards Soho."

Soho: "I've seen them here twice before, and they camped in the same place by the river. They are the travelling people, probably the Drummonds or the Stewarts from outside Stornoway."

Iain: "The travelling people, sometimes referred to as tinkers, are people skilled in the use of tin, making or repairing pots from tin or tinplate. They are often called Highland tinkers, and move camp from place to place in the months of spring and summer. The Gaelic for tinker is *'ceard'*, but the word has been so misused by some people, that the tinkers themselves dislike this word. They are not that keen on the name 'tinker', for much the same reason, and prefer to be called travellers." The two cats, Soho and Rupie, followed Iain down the *leathadh,* and they headed towards the *traigh* to speak with the tinkers, if that was possible. One got the feeling that Iain knew these people, because frankly, *'An 'Houdie* knew everyone (almost).

Iain: "Seamus Drummond, I believe?"

Drummond: "Yes, Seamus Drummond, and that is my wife and children, and some of the grandparents. We'll be in the Carloway district for the next week. We haven't been here for a few years, so I suspect that we will be able to sell some new tin pails and mugs, and repair any old ones that are leaking."

Rupie: "You don't seem to have any cats here with you, only dogs."

Drummond: "We never take cats on our travels. Cats prefer a settled existence and our three stay in our home in Stornoway. But, come over and meet the dogs, Cormac the Irish wolfhound and Billy the border terrier. You are quite safe - are they not, boys?" Tentatively, Rupie and Soho approached the dogs and were surprised to see Cormac and Billy offer up a *spog* for them to shake. Even Iain Shoudie had never witnessed such amazing animal behaviour. Cormac was a giant of a dog who towered over Soho and Rupie, but his calm demeanour and measured movements put our cats at their ease. His hair was long and grey and he had bushy eyebrows and a neat beard. The wolfhounds had been the hunting dogs favoured by the ancient Irish kings. The border terrier was a *braw* wee lad, who went everywhere with his big pal, Cormac. Billy loved this gentle giant and he looked up to him, in more ways than one.

Cormac: "Of course, we hope your dog friends will feel free to visit us here in camp."

Iain: "Of course, Seamus, pots and pans is not your only business. You are famous for trading in horses, and buying quality scrap metal."

Drummond: "Absolutely. As they say 'Man cannot live by bread alone'. In our case, we can no longer survive solely on our traditional skills. The world is moving on, and we must move with the times. Yes, we buy certain metals, and in this village, for example, there is a young lad who trades with us in those metal floats which detach from fishermen's nets at sea. I buy them from him at a shilling a time, and sell them on to the fishermen in Stornoway, at a profit of course. Most of the horses bought and sold in Lewis are traded through us. In fact, tomorrow I am going to see a horse in Upper

Carloway, and you are welcome to come along. If it is as good as they say it is, then I have a mind to buy the horse."

The following day, Seamus Drummond, with his son Angus, stopped to pick up Iain Shoudie and the dogs, Stowlia, Fancy, Jura and Fred in his little lorry, which he happened to call the 'pickup'- a very appropriate name, thought Jura. With Cormac and Billy already in the back of the pickup, the addition of the Dalmore dogs made for a barking mad and excitable crew as they passed through Carloway. When they reached their destination, they all caught sight of this magnificent chestnut horse, a young stallion in full gallop in a field by the road. Cormac intimated that he was pretty sure that Seamus would buy this beautiful horse, if the price was right. Seamus gave the horse careful scrutiny, looking at his teeth and hind quarters and there was also some mention of fetlocks and withers, which must have been important to Seamus, but which even 'An 'Houdie had never heard of before. The price was agreed, and Seamus asked his son to lead the horse back to Dalmore. A few days later, when they went down to see the Drummonds, Seamus was making new pails and mugs from sheets of tinplate.

Cormac: "I think that you'll find this interesting, folks. Seamus uses the shears to cut out the shapes of tin he needs. He uses these metal compasses to form circular shapes for the bottom of the pail or jug, and special cone shaped anvils to form the sides of the various vessels. He does this using a hammer with a leather covered head."

Billy: "That small lump of silver-coloured metal is called solder which is used to join the various parts together. The soldering iron is heated in the fire and when applied to the solder with some soldering paste (called 'flux') the solder melts and is guided along the seam with the iron. The solder must be lead-free as the vessels will carry items of food. The 'raw' top edge of the pail or jug is 'rolled' to remove its sharp edge and finally a hooked handle is attached to finish the tin vessel."

Jura: "They are very skilled, the travellers, at what they do and I don't believe they would change their way of life for any other."

Iain: "Now, Seamus, a lot of people are afraid of travellers. They say that you ask people for food for your children, and being afraid that a refusal would result in a curse on them or their home, people do your bidding."

Seamus: "It is true that some travellers have played on the superstitions of people that we can *'put the spog on them'*. They confuse us with the Gypsies or Romany who did claim these powers. We don't have these powers and I doubt if the Romany have them either. I think people see us as an alien race, with a different life and customs, and are a bit wary of us. We have lived the travellers' life now for generations, and will continue to do so into the future. No one needs to have any fear of us. We will be leaving tomorrow, and you're all invited down here tomorrow evening for a bite to eat. I hope you can come."

Iain Shoudie: "*Dha-riribh*, we will be there, Seamus."

The following night, Iain and Murdo with their retinue of dogs and cats joined the Drummond family around the large fire in front of the tents. Mrs Drummond and her eldest daughter had prepared various small cakes and other sweetmeats. Seamus produced a bottle of malt whisky which found favour with '*Balaich Shoudie*'. There was much talk and laughter around the fire that night and the animals entered the spirit of the occasion, playing games that were taught to young travellers (and their animals) from time immemorial. As the evening drew to a close, Seamus pointed in the direction of the *traigh* and, with the help of the light from the roaring fire, all could see young Angus Drummond riding the young stallion in their direction. Everyone cheered the young rider and his beautiful chestnut horse. The night was almost over, but there was one more surprise in store for the company. Again, looking towards the sea, they could hear something approaching but couldn't make out what it was in the darkness. Suddenly, lit by the fire, they were amazed to see Billy the terrier riding towards them on the back of his friend, Cormac, very steady at an even trot. There was uproar and applause at this humorous jape. There were fond goodbyes that night, but they all resolved to get together when the Drummonds came again to Dalmore.

Taigh 'Houdie - the Shoudie's house

"A'Ghille, thoir suil air sinn" – O', boy, have a look at that

braw (Scots) – handsome

put the spog on them - curse them

dha-riridh – indeed

Balaich Shoudie - the Shoudie boys.

Making Hay and Old Stories

It had been another warm day. This was the fourth day of glorious weather, which elsewhere would not be deemed unusual but in Dalmore, even in July, this was exceptional. The air was warm and balmy and the smell of cut hay hung heavily over the *feannaigean*. Clover flowers gave off a delicate perfume, and the bees were ever busy gathering nectar. The sky was a pale blue with a few cirrus clouds seemingly motionless, high in the firmament. Down at the *traigh* the sea was azure blue and no sound was heard, but for the few small rollers to reach the beach. On a day like this, Dalmore really is God's Little Acre. The animals from *Taigh Shoudie* and the *Taigh Glass* animals had worked hard at the hay making, Iain Shoudie had said, but their contribution was of a specialised nature. They caught the mice (and a few rats) which fled the advancing cuts of the scythe. They carried their fellow creatures to a place of safety, and there released them. This was a policy now favoured by them all, called 'catch and release'. Fred, the wee Glasgow terrier, could not get his head round this. It was against nature, he said, and certainly against his nature. Still, when in Dalmore, do as the Romans do. The ministrations of the Reverend MacCollie had won over the hearts of his Dalmore 'flock'. They now lay on the hay, tired but happy, and it was not long before they fell asleep in the shade of a hay stack. Filax, Victoria, Rupie and So-Sally, the cats, were asleep lying close to one another, while the dogs, Stowlia, Fancy, Jura and Fred were lying on a bundle of hay near the top of the *feannaig*. Shonnie and 'An 'Houdie were good with the *speal* and had cut a fair amount of hay that day. The hay would be turned in the following days using pitchforks and rakes, to ensure that it was thoroughly dry before it was taken by cart to the barn.

After their rest, Fancy suggested a climb to the top of the Beinn Dhalamor above *Taigh Glass*, which afforded a magnificent view of the village and beyond. The highest point on the Beinn is an outcrop called Clach Thormaid, and no one knows why this large boulder, stranded here during the Ice Age, is called Norman's stone. Fancy offered himself as guide, this being his own backyard, and suggested that he might mention a few stories, which he had heard in *Taigh Glass* in the past.

Fancy: "The dark, dank, passage we passed through has taken us part of the way up the *beinn*. It is known to this day as Sgorr Dhomhnull Duncan, and it is said that it was here that this man, Domhnull Duncan, chose to say his prayers. He was at that time a shepherd on the Dalmore/Dalbeg sheep farm, run by the Sinclair family from their house in Dalbeg. The people in these villages were cleared from their homes about 100 years ago to make way for many hundreds of Cheviot sheep, which would enrich the tacksman, but disinherit and impoverish the people of the *Dailean*. Domhnull Duncan was devoutly religious, and a man credited with the second sight. One day, while walking on the Beinn, he was amazed and a little afraid as he looked down at the valley below. Where he might have expected to see a land ravished by hundreds of sheep, he now saw fields of potatoes and others of corn and barley gently swaying in the breeze. When he reported this strange spectacle to Old Mistress Sinclair back in the farmhouse in Dalbeg, it is said that tears filled her eyes. She knew that their days here were over."

Rupie: "Since the time of the clearances from the two villages and throughout the years of the sheep farm, up until the land was set aside as crofts, this was a period of 60 years. Kenny Iceland claims that one day while emerging from a rabbit burrow, he beheld Dalmore 60 years into the future. He makes no claims of being a seer, but what he saw that day was real enough and, is in his mind, a portent of a time to come. He saw a glen where no crops grow, where sheep have returned in even greater numbers and where the land is not green, but grey, *odhar* you might say. He saw the land again raped by the Big Sheep, as it had been following the clearance in 1850. Neither Padraig Sinclair nor Sir James Matheson can be blamed for what Kenny Iceland saw that day. The future Dalmore made a pitiful spectacle, in which today's industry and thrift would be replaced by greed and indolence. And yet, when we look down on the beautiful village now, it is hard to believe what Kenny saw but, like *Cailleach* Sinclair's response to Domhnull Duncan's prophecy, one day we too might have tears in our eyes, but for different reasons."

That evening in *Taigh 'Houdie*, the animals were gathered round the fire, listening to Old Murdo telling stories and, as often is the case, the stories gravitated to ghosts and the 'second sight.' After some time, Murdo hushed his excited little friends.

Murdo: "People somehow believe that ghosts only existed in the distant past and that nowadays we never hear anything about them. But that is not the case, and to prove the point listen to this story about events which happened only 30 years ago in a village near here. It concerns a widow lady called Mary, who died a few months after buying a cow from a man in her own village. She was buried in the cemetery here in Dalmore but some time later strange things began to happen, which frightened the villagers. Mary could be seen walking through the village, still dressed in her burial shroud, with her eyes fixed pitifully on people as if she wanted them to stop her and to speak to her. Word soon spread and people were terrified of the unearthly spectre of a woman whose burial they attended only weeks before. For days Mary walked down the road through the village, but no one dared speak to her. However, one day, a man who had lived next to her during her life, saw Mary approach and addressed her as follows:

Man: 'Mary, why in God's name do you still walk this earth, when I know that you died, and saw you buried in Dalmore?'

Mary: 'My soul is greatly troubled, and I will not rest easy until my name has been cleared of the vile rumour that has been spread about me among the good people of our village. You will remember that I bought a cow from Duncan, some weeks before I died, and he now claims that I did not pay for it, and is claiming the money from my relatives. What he says is a lie, and I cannot rest in my grave unless the truth is told. If you go to my house, you will find under a lamp on the dresser, a paper which is the receipt for the sale of the cow.'

The man found the receipt, confronted Duncan, and Mary was never seen again."

speal – scythe

odhar – dull, dark

cailleach - old woman

Dailean - dales

ON THE CREST OF A WAVE

"*A bhalaich*" shouted Iain 'Houdie, "*thoir suil air a mhachair.*"
His brother Murdo came out of the *taigh dubh* in a hurry,
followed by Stowlia, Soho and Rupie who, in their haste,
knocked over a creel and an old milk churn *anns a chuil
mhoine*. Their view over Dalmore was the complete panorama,
as *Taigh 'Houdie* was located so high up under the Beinn.
With an uninterrupted view of the shore, what assailed their
eyes was simply incredible. People were walking on top of the
waves, not swimming, not sailing, actually walking. They
were standing up as they walked on the waves, looking for all
like men in charge of several white horses. Of course,
everyone knew of the One who had walked on the waters a
long time ago, but no one expected this feat to be repeated
again, and certainly not here in Dalmore. Iain and Murdo
were, it has to be said, a little afraid, as were the animals, but
this was no mirage. There was a group of people, some
walking on the waves while others seem to be swallowed by
the waves, only to reappear once more on top. No matter
what, it was decided to take a walk down to the *traigh* and
take a closer look.

As they passed the 'turning point' at the road's end, they saw
this long narrow van parked opposite the cemetery gate. It
was painted with strange designs, in loud garish colours and
over its body work were many stickers advertising the places
the van had visited - foreign sounding names like Bondi,
Nanahoa, Biarritz and Malibu. Even *'An 'Houdie* in his years
at sea had never heard of these strange places. And to stick
names on your van, well? Seoras would look pretty silly if he
were to stick 'Timisgarry' or 'Portnaguran' on the side of his

wee Austin van and he had been to those places. The curiosity of our party grew, with every step they took towards the *traigh*. When the sea came in view, they witnessed the most fantastic circus, people performing acts of great beauty and skill, on and under the large waves that ploughed relentlessly towards the beach. Stowlia looked at *'An 'Houdie* in disbelief, and soon they all sat down on the warm sand to witness a most amazing display. There were four people out there on the waves and had they not been standing or

crouching, they could easily have been mistaken for seals in their shiny black skins. After a while, the four 'seals' were carried to the shore on the smaller waves. They were lying full length on large curved boards, which they paddled to the shore, using their hands. As they walked up the beach, carrying these strange boards under their arms, you could see from their shape that the seals were in fact two men and two women. When they started to get out of their skins, *Iain 'Houdie* had to calm his friends, who went ballistic with their howling and caterwauling. *"Istibh a' charaidean*, can't you see they that they are just men and women, not monsters from the deep." Fred was relieved. This big guy came towards the group in his underpants (poor man) and his body all over was the colour of a lightly smoked kipper, though to be fair, there was no smell.

Offering his hand to Iain, he said "G'day, my name is Shane and I come from Australia." "Hello, Shine, my name is John, and I come from Dalmore." This tall Australian was amazed to see each of the Dalmore crew offering him a friendly *spog*, which the big fella gently shook. "Struth, mate, we don't have such cute little animals back home." Wait till he discovered that these little cuties could also speak! "Let me introduce my friends. This is my mucker, Jason, and these two beauties are Kimberley and Shannon." Each were the colour of a kipper, but for all that, they were tall, blond and handsome. Jason too was in his underpants like Shane, but *'An 'Houdie* noticed that these pants had no *sper* (very strange). The young ladies wore bathing suits, the likes of which had never graced Dalmore beach before. No woman from Dalmore was likely to possess a bathing suit, since none of them could swim or felt the need to. There must have been a shortage of cloth in Australia (perhaps war rationing was still in place) as the ladies' bathing suits had a top part, a bottom part (no pun intended) but there was nothing in between. Iain thought that it would be fun to see Bantrach Aonghas Seumas in a suit like this with the Orb stamped on the bottom. *Iain 'Houdie* had an active imagination, at times best kept to himself. Fred had a few questions for the young Australians.

Fred: "What were you doing out there on the sea, and what magic allows you to travel so fast on top of the waves and standing up at that?"

Shane: "No, Fred, we were not walking on the waters; we were surfing the waves, as we say. These long boards allow us to ride on the crest of a wave, and the idea is to stay on board (another pun!) as long as we can. For protection we wear those 'wet suits'. Like most things, your surfing skills improve with practice, but I have to say that surfing is better in places where the weather is warm and the waves are high, places like Australia where we come from, or California and South Africa. People can spend a lot of money having their surf boards specially designed for them."

Fred: "Shane, do you think we could learn to surf if we practised?"

Shane: "What we can do is to take you out on the waves with us, and we'll see how it goes. We will probably have to keep a hold of you or, if you're brave, you can hold onto our feet down at the surf board. So what do you say, cobber?"

Before Fred could reply, there was an outcry from the rest that answered Shane's question.

Kimberley: "If you guys come back around six, we'll have a kick-out, and maybe we'll have something to throw on the barbie."

So-Sally: "Kick-out? I don't think so! And no one is going to throw me on a barbie, whatever that is."

Six o'clock and they were all down on the *traigh* to see some very high rollers heading their way. Kimberley and Shannon were already in their wet suits and were standing in the surf holding their boards. So-Sally and Filax were the first to take to the waves with the Aussie girls, who held them high as the boards carried our intrepid *piseagean* across the bay at speed. So-Sally and Filax were transported, deliriously happy, if a little wet. So-Sally didn't give the kick-out a second thought. Fancy (with aviator goggles) and Fred, being dogs of course (well, of course) elected for the more daring option of sitting on the surf boards holding on to the feet of the boys. Shane and Jason, lying flat on their boards began paddling out through the surf to a point where the larger waves were forming, no easy matter with a dog on your back, hanging on to your 'shorts' for all its worth. At a prearranged signal, Shane and Jason stood up to surf the big waves and Fred and Fancy held on the boys' feet as if their life depended on it - it did actually. "*O bhobh, bhobh*", cried Fancy, while Fred shouted "Go on, yersel, Wee Man." The surfing boys were enjoying themselves, and were determined to give their 'wee pals' the experience of a life time, riding their boards on the crest of the waves. Even Fancy began to relax, although she couldn't see much through her water-logged goggles (a blessing, perhaps). They were *kicking out, walking the nose* and using the *wind swells.* Then they started the most terrifying manoeuvres of all; riding through the *barrel waves.* Jason and Shane told the pals to hold on tight as they were about enter a long tunnel of water. Man, O Man, as they sped through this long barrel wave it was as though they were in world of green, blue crystal glass, through which you could see the sky and the white clouds above. Finally they came ashore, soaked and exhilarated. They thanked their friends for a wonderful time, and encouraged the rest of the gang to try their hand at surfing.

Kimberley and Shannon took over, and everyone was amazed to see Victoria, the beautifully coiffed blue-cream Persian cat, riding out onto the waves holding Shannon's ankle very tightly. Fred asked to have another go at surfing, this time with Kimberley, who was happy to oblige. He held on to her legs very tightly as they passed through two successive barrel waves. The young Australians had explained to Iain and Murdo all about the 'barbie' they were arranging for later on, down by the *allt.* Shannon, it was revealed, is an accomplished diver and earlier that day had caught some large crabs and two lobsters out at the point near the 'Man's Head'. John had caught some saithe yesterday over at Bandaberie and this would be cooked on the barbie along with Shannon's shellfish. The barbecue (barbie, in Australian) was made from a number of large round stones, in which the peats burned and, lying across everything, was a large metal grill on which the fish, crabs and lobsters would be cooked. The food was continually turned on the barbie and what resulted was some of the sweetest fare that you could have imagined. Shane remarked how the peat smoke had enhanced the flavour of the food and Murdo and Iain thought that Atlantic chilled lager added something to the taste of the lobster. The Dalmore crew were used to eating saithe, but who could have imagined sitting on this golden beach eating crab and lobster as the red sun set in the West.

There were a few more peats thrown on the barbie and a few more tinnies despatched before everyone parted as friends. It was unlikely that a surf board would ever again be seen on Traigh Dhalamor, but Kenny Iceland was not so sure. Last night he had a dream.

A bhalaich, thoir suil air a mhachair - Boys, take a look at the beach

anns a chuil mhoine - in the corner peat store

Seoras - George

Istibh a' charaidean - Be quiet, friends

sper - front opening of trousers

Bantrach Aonghas Seumas - Angus James's Widow

piseagean – kittens

O bhobh, bhobh - O, dear, dear

SHAWBOST GAMES

Carloway could boast of its prestigious Agricultural Show, and lately its Football Team had achieved some success, under the inspired management of the 'Bear'. He had adopted the trainer's use of the wet sponge which at that time was looked on as the cure-all for all knocks, aches and pains. Massey and Tormod Nelson were among the first players to feel the cold of the wet sponge. The Bear also had a pail of orange juice, which immediately conferred legitimacy on him as trainer/manager. If truth be told, some of the stalwarts of Carloway F.C. actually came from Shawbost. Shawbost was a no-nonsense sort of a place with a secondary school, a large tweed mill and its highly esteemed Free Church. You will remember that Shawbost was also the location of the Avian Free Church, which was the largest animal church in the Isle of Lewis, possibly in all the Hebrides. So Shawbost had a lot going for it, and the residents, animal or otherwise, were rightly proud of their village. The Shawbost Sheepdog Trials, held each summer, were claimed to be second only to Stornoway's in the island's rankings. In the parallel world of the animals, this was always the day when competing cats, dogs and birds foregathered at *Creag an Fheidh* which is a flat plain between the north end of Beinn Bhragair and the hill known as Cleite Rathailt. This was a day of sports and celebration, when the most talented animals demonstrated their prowess and speed, or in other ways entertained the vast throng of spectators out there on the moor behind Shawbost.

The 'games' were supported with subsidies and grants, in the acquisition of which the Reverend MacCraw of the local Avian Free Church was foremost. The large animal charities like SSPCA and the RSPB were quickly off the mark in supporting the games, which in their view were unique. Coinneach Rodd, the local tweed mill owner, made a substantial donation. Some say that Torcuil, his magnificent Scottish deer hound, had a say in his master's benevolence. If truth be told, the animal 'stadium' at Creag an Fheidh was well appointed, with artificial tree stumps and cinder beds provided for the animals' comfort. No special arrangements were required for the birds. For them it was 'take your ease where you please'.

Dogs, cats and birds made their way to Shawbost from every village in Lewis, and probably beyond. The dogs and cats had staggered arrival times, insisted on by the police, and nearer their venues they were directed down different routes. The dogs posed one extra problem: dogs might be competing at the sheep dog trials or simply heading for the games. As Stowlia said, chasing sheep is not every dog's 'thing' - why should it be? The local constabulary were on top of all matters relating to crowd control. All birds, competing or otherwise, simply flew in to Creag an Fheidh, no policing required.

The games were formally opened by the Reverend MacCraw, who surprised everyone with an uplifting speech and a short pithy prayer. The games had begun. There were no mixed events between the three species; three species because, remember, dogs who didn't chase sheep could nevertheless enter for the FAC Games. The official designation of the Shawbost games was **F** (feline), **A** (avian) and **C** (canine). Mr MacCraw thought they stood a better chance of a subsidy or grant if they adopted the impressive acronym, FAC.

The running events mainly involved the dogs and cats, and it has to be said that the home grown *coin is cait* took the main honours. Big Torcuil, the Scottish deer hound, swept the boards at the canine cross-country and the Shorter Marathon (from Creag an Fheidh to the nearest point of Loch Raoinabhat and back). In the feline running events, there was an obvious correlation between youth, low body weight, and success. For some unfathomable reason, black cats predominated. The vast majority of animal competitors were lean and extremely fit, but one very large tabby cat, from Bragair I think, was referred to as 'obese' but no one understood this word, coming as it did from a teacher from the Nicolson, who was wont to using long or abstruse words. 'Obese' indeed!

The policing inside the stadium was not done by the local constabulary, but was handled by a team of around fifty members of the crow family. They were impressive, dressed as they were in black cotton blousons, orange berets and all wearing dark glasses in case the sun came out. They called themselves The West Side Crew. To our Dalmore team, The West Side Crew could only be described as *annasach*, an unusual concept in policing whose members bore the word SECURITY on the back of their jackets. So-Sally and Rupie were fascinated with the crew, their demeanour, and their language. They were doing an excellent job inside and outside the stadium. So-Sally recognised their 'main man' who was constantly consulted by the other crows, and from whom all orders came. Whispering to Rupie from behind her *spogs*, she identified him as the crow they met on the road to Shawbost when they attended the *reitich* of Eilidh (Helen) and Uisdean (Hugh) some time ago. He was the tall shiny crow who appeared from behind a *cruach*, wearing a multi-segmented leather cap and a scarf of many colours. He spoke in a strange way, addressing them as 'beeches' and asking them 'what was going down'. Well, here he was now, confidently in charge of fifty odd security crows, all of whom spoke the same patois as their boss, whom they always addressed as Daddyo.

"I'm so happy for the lad. Something bad happened to him out in Glasgow, but now he seems fine", said Rupie. "*Mo bheannachd air*", added Soho.

The big birds were now competing in the favourite event 'Tossing the Haddock over the Bar' in which the last three surviving contestants were a golden eagle from Uig, a buzzard from Lochs and a giant gull from Five Penny, Ness. The contest was suddenly stopped when the Ness gull was eliminated for eating the haddock, after what was probably the winning throw - probably the excitement, they said.

There were many heats before the feline sprint finals took place. Against expectations, Aonghais Ruadh's big ginger tom from Dalbeg tore through the field to lift two gold medals (gold foil, actually). The dogs taking part in the *maide leisg* were very competitive, even aggressive. Their *spogs* were often wrongly placed to gain an advantage over their opponent but this was picked up by the referee, Tormod Laidir, who was a past champion in this ancient sport. Our friends from Dalmore were enjoying themselves immensely, and endeavoured to remain close to, and within earshot of the crows from The West Side Crew. They were bamboozled, yet fascinated by their strange talk. Daddyo asked Rupie, straight out, if she was a 'square or a cool cat'. How does a wee cat from Dalmore answer that? Another Crew member was saying that Loch Raoinabhat would soon be where the action was at saying "It's gonna be a blast over there, really far out". "It's going to be the coolest happening, man - let's split the scene here," said Daddyo, with the hint of a Lewis accent. Stowlia was puzzled, and asked So-Sally what these crows were talking about. Soho threw her *spogs* in the air, before replying, "*A' ghraidh, Chan eil cail a dh'fhios agam.*"

It transpired that the closing events of the games were about to take place over on Loch Raoinabhat. The vast crowds standing on the banks of the loch were amazed at what they saw. Out on the loch were mallard ducks and Canada geese giving an amazing display of synchronised paddling. They would weave in and out of each other, and simultaneously would plunge their necks into the waters, leaving their rear-ends high in the air, shaking in unison.

The final event involved a spectacular display of aerial manoeuvres from the birds of prey. Finally, everyone could see, rising above Dalbeg and coming in over the west end of the loch, a formation of eagles, buzzards and falcons, coming towards them at speed and just above the waves. In pole position, and slightly ahead of the others, was Gillesbuig, our local eagle from Beinn Bhragair. They didn't have this at the Carloway Show - did they?

By the way, Tiger Navarre's dog Toss won the Sheep Dog Trials.

Creag an Fheidh - Deer rock

coin is cait - dogs and cats

annasach – strange, rare, unusual

cruach – peat stack

Mo bheannachd air - Blessings on him

maide leisg - "the lazy stick"

Tormod Laidir - Norman the Strong

A' ghraidh, Chan eil cail a dh'fhios agam - I haven't the faintest idea, my dear

THE ROAD

If you live by the sea, there is something with which you will be very familiar. I refer to the tides, high and low, of which even the animals are aware. Murdo explained to his friends that it was caused by the pull of the moon and the sun on the waters of the earth's oceans. He mentioned 'gravity' but now the explanation was getting right complicated, flying right over our heads, even for the tallest among us.

Recently, it was noticed that the low tides down at the *traigh* at Dalmore, were getting very low indeed and that the sea was very far out. It was now possible to walk across to the Gearraidh where the sea would normally be and a day or two later, the sea was out beyond Rudha an Trilleachain and all the *geodhain* and *stacan* were now totally accessible, where normally they were below the sea and battered by powerful waves. Murdo said something about the sun, the moon and our earth being in line with each other and it was this that caused these very low tides. A tide like this was called a 'Road' and we were never sure that this name was used anywhere else. Fancy reckoned that it was a perfectly good name, as the withdrawal of the sea gave you a road where there hadn't been one before. Fair enough! Soho ventured that you could only get a Road where the *traigh's* sandy beach sloped gently out to sea. Soho was recently visiting friends near the Big Sands at Uig and she said she saw a large lorry full of peats motoring across the sandy bay there, which only a few hours earlier had been covered by the incoming waves.

When you looked out from where the *traigh* normally lies, it gave you an eerie feeling that the sea had disappeared and it might return no more. Rupie looked to Murdo for reassurance, who told them all that the sea would come back again. He remembered reading about such things in a National Geographic magazine, which a visitor had left with him.

"Would it be possible to walk all around the coast to Garenin, where the sea used to be?", asked Fancy. "I'm not sure about that, but it might be possible. But we will stay here on Traigh Dhalamor, and see what happens", replied Murdo.

In the next few days, there was a lot of activity on the *traigh*. Stowlia stayed close to 'An 'Houdie, who was laying his "*loidhne bheag*" across the dry sandy beach, attached to those of Seoras and Shonnie. That amounted to a lot of 'hyooks' all baited with herring and the idea was to catch small flounders that bury themselves in the sand when the tide returns.

"So the tide comes in after all. We thought that the seas stayed away out there for days," said Fred, looking at Seoras, having heard he was a bit of a sage.

Seoras told him that the tides still operated, but to a lesser extent; the low tide was very low, and the high tide was not as high as usual, only coming into the *traigh* part way. That's where the fishing lines were set.

"Do you see how simply Seoras explained the tides. That's the mark of the sage," said Soho.

For the women of the village, and the children, an important reason for being down at the *traigh* was to harvest *siolan*, which they could not do at other times. Siolan are known also as sand-eels or whitebait which, when disturbed, can use their long pointed noses to disappear beneath the sand. Siolan are the fish you see arranged so neatly along the colourful beak of the puffin. Equipped with a *corran* and a tin pail, we see the people pulling the *corran* through the wet sand. When the blade comes into contact with a sand-eel (It is in fact a fish), you search down with an open hand to catch the silver *siolan*. You can fill buckets and pails with these fish, and if they are full, then it's into the pockets of your overalls. They make very tasty fish soup.

Stowlia, Fancy and Fred joined in this fish free-for-all, but not with any great success. Fred, however, being a terrier, could dig furiously and did score a few times, casually flicking the fish towards his feline friends, now in raptures of delight with their hero, the 'Wee Glesca' Man'. Nevertheless, their excitement was palpable as they watched their human friends fill one pail after another with those beautiful silver fish. Seoras remembered that when he was a young man in Dalmore, there would be people with their horse and cart far out on the *traigh*, collecting seaweed which would later be used as fertiliser. We collected the *duileasg* and *bairneach*, while others harvested great quantities of *claba-dubha*, favoured in Shawbost and points North.

All the Dalmore cats and dogs got into the spirit of thing, racing about on the new-found sands, splashing about in the long sea pools, abandoned by the tide. To see Vicky, our immaculate blue cream Persian cat, splashing Soho and Filax with the deft use of her back-*spogs*, was a delight to behold. The animals might be wet and covered in sand, but they were truly happy.

Up on the *machair* grass beside the *allt*, some of the women had a large peat fire going. They had a large iron pot, into which all the ingredients for the fish soup were placed - the *siolan* of course, onion, water and a little milk and butter. This was an outdoor kitchen, and the fish soup (we called it '*souse*') just kept coming! How I remember the taste of that soup.

When the small lines were lifted later the following day, there was a good catch of *leabagain*, and a few other species of fish. The catch was of course divided equally among Seoras, Shonnie and 'An 'Houdie. There was no boat share and this must be one of the few occasions where this happens.

The Road eventually ran its course and before the sea returned to normal levels, it had given of its many bounties. And with that, life in Dalmore was to return to normality. One evening in *Taigh 'Houdie*, when all had partaken of another fish feast, Murdo said that he was minded of a lovely story about another Road, but not on the sea. There must have been a dozen animals looking up at Murdo in eager anticipation of this tale, as he had what people called '*blas*' in his story telling (literally 'taste' - a tasty tale).

Murdo: "This is a true story which involved my father, Shoudie, when he was a young man living in Garenin. He was sitting down by the *cladach*, with two of his friends, Tormod Anna and Long (Glass's brother), doing nothing in particular but enjoying it just the same. They saw this man, a stranger from his garb, approaching them from the direction of the Gleann. He must have been at Borriston or Laimishadair and they quickly had him down as one of these commercial travellers one sees from time to time. The man addressed them in English and asked them where the main road was, to Stornoway presumably.

Shoudie, shaking his head from side to side, shouted 'Naw-thing, Naw-thing' and the man understood. Tormod Anna asked a favour *"A dhuine uasail, a' bheil siucar iad?"* ('Sir, have you got a sweetie?'). Bless him! Long said 'The Rathad Mor is up-a-bitty, up-a-bitty. It's coming up again'. Gesturing with his hand, Long showed the traveller how he could connect with the main road at Carloway. The man thanked the three Garenin lads, who returned to take their ease."

The assembled company loved Murdo's story, as always, and they too returned to take their ease. Not much has changed, then.

> *geodhain* - creeks
>
> *stacan* - stacks
>
> *loidhne bheag* - small (fishing) line
>
> *corran* – sickle
>
> *duileasg* – red dulse
>
> *bairneach* – limpets
>
> *claba-dubha* – mussels
>
> *leabagain* – small sole
>
> *cladach* – shore

ORDAIGHEAN SIABOST
(SHAWBOST'S COMMUNIONS)

It was that time again. There were noticeable and unusual movements of people and animals throughout Lewis. Buses were transporting hundreds of people dressed in dark clothing, to various places around the island. At first glance, one might think that they were destined for some distant funeral.

There was a certain gravitas about these people and inside the bus there hung the strange odour of camphor and peppermint. As the bus passed through various townships, the people did not talk, and the silence was broken only occasionally by the rustling of paper. The driver certainly had a destination in mind and was aware of the nature of this journey. The people were mainly old in age, but not exclusively. Hard toil and a harsh climate were etched on their faces and here their Sunday clothes seemed strangely out of place. However, any onlooker might underrate the strength of character of the people who travelled in that bus, some perhaps sucking quietly on a Mint Imperial.

Any *Leodhhasach* would know that this was the season of Communions called *Na Ordaighean*, held in all the churches across the island. It is a unique Presbyterian season, consisting of various services including the sacrament of communion. All are welcome to these services, but only the worthy can approach the table to partake of the bread and wine. These communicants are known as *comanaiche*, and are often described as *curamach*. Those who do take communion are known among their brethren as committed to their Lord. It is a very public affirmation of their faith, and is never taken lightly. It was because of *Na Ordaighean* that Presbyterian manses were built so large, to accommodate visiting ministers at such times.

The animal churches had always synchronised their communions with those of their human kind. If you knew that there were communions in Shawbost, for example, then you could be sure that *Na Ordaighean Eaglais na Eoin* were being held in Shawbost too. Dogs and cats from the Doune church were welcome here in Shawbost, despite being of a 'different denomination'. Among the animals and birds, the word 'denomination' was borrowed long ago from man's lexicon, but now it was meaningless and of little import in the animals' doctrine of faith. The animal churches were an example of the ecumenism that had long eluded the 'man churches' in Lewis. Theirs was a history of dissent and schism, which baffled the animal congregations. At the animal communions one might expect a great, if not incongruous, mix of communicants sitting side by side in the pews - the eagle with the lamb or the cat with the sparrow. The elders of *Eaglais na Eoin* had wisely anticipated the problems which could arise by dint of hunger or an animal's natural instincts and they did all they could to allay the fears of the small and the timid among their flock. Animals were matched in size and temperament in the various services, although there would always be a problem with the golden eagles.

The Dalmore crew were fairly regular churchgoers, with the exception of Kenny Iceland and Tom Warrener who long ago had foregone the comforts of home for the cold and damp of the rabbit burrows. You would only see them on the odd occasion if the hunting was poor or the weather was foul. They had no idea what day it was, and wouldn't know if it was a Sunday, assuming that they had a mind to go to church at all, which they normally didn't. Fancy was out at the *geata iarran* this Wednesday evening, when he espied three dark figures making their way in the Dalmore road. Positioning himself behind a peat stack, closer examination revealed that it was the Reverend MacCollie with two large dogs, probably elders in the Doune church. Forewarned, Fancy sped ahead to the village to announce the imminent arrival of these dogs of doom.

MacCollie and his cohorts stopped a few times as they went in the road to talk to the odd cat or upbraid some poor dog for his irregular attendance at church - leaving the poor soul with a 'hung dog' expression across his face. MacCollie was in his usual garb of large dog collar, long dark coat and the obligatory Homburg hat on his head. His elders were dressed in dark attire, and walked a few paces behind MacCollie, in a *crub* posture. The Doune churchmen looked as if they had walked straight off the pages of Revelations. Kenny Iceland in *Taigh 'Houdie* maintained that he had heard The Horses of the Apocalypse out at the Mullach Mor. We must remember that Kenny was credited with the second sight.

Rupie: "And what kind of horses are they? Are they like Jimmy, or *Each na Cnaimhan*? "

Soho: "No, *a' ghraidh*, much bigger, you could say, but don't you worry yourself."

Iain and Murdo, *Balaich 'Houdie*, were seated on the *leathad* down from the house' with their animals seated around them, when the minister and his elders approached.

Iain: "*Madainn mhath, a' Mhinister. De tha a dhith oiribh?*"

MacCollie: "A courtesy call, *'An 'Houdie*, just passing through."

Elder no. 1: "*Dha riribh, a' dhaoine, dha riribh.*"

Stowlia noted that Iain used that same phrase a lot, but as often, he exaggerated it to sound like 'gha reeroo'.

Soho: "Mr MacCollie, rest assured that we'll be attending a service in Shawbost. Isn't that right, folks?"

In unison the others answered *'dha riribh, dha riribh'.*

Fred: "Take a gander at him wi' the big stick. He's a bear of a man. Is he the Witchfinder General or the Wicker Man? He scares the hell outa me."

He was referring to Elder no. 2, whose eyes were fixed on Kenny Iceland.

MacCollie: "Kenny, It's been many a year since I saw you in church. Are you not afraid for your immortal soul? The communions are on at the moment and we are on our way to the Wednesday evening prayer meeting in Shawbost. We'd like you to come with us."

Kenny: "You pray for Shawbost if you like, *A' Mhinister*, but I am staying right here in Dalmore"

MacCollie: "Many in our flock have taken the *curam* at these meetings. They have been collapsing in raptures - even Gilleasbuig the golden eagle.

Fred: "A' widnae like to be anywhere near the Big Man when he collapsed. I remember a few years ago in the Kelvin Hall in Glasgow when the American evangelist, Uilleam Greumach, was calling on thousands to come forward to be saved. I made to join the throng of howling animals, when my brother grabbed me by the tail and said. 'Sit doon, Fred. If you join that lot, there will be no more raids on the Lucky Midgies, doon the Double Dykes'. I could never fault my brother's advice!

Fancy: "I think Kenny is a Pantheist. We should respect him for that."

Mr MacCollie smiled, bid farewell and left.

Ordaighean Siabost were a great success. The Reverend MacCraw, Macraw Mor, was on his home turf and his preaching was as powerful as anyone can remember. When he spoke to the book of Isaiah, the very rafters shook. Here at the communions, there had been powerful sermonising, intelligent discourse on doctrine and the articles of faith, and very many conversions. The greatest of these was surely that of the big eagle from Beinn Bhragair. The example of his faith would be carried higher and further than ever before. The buses left for Doune and other villages, and the peppermint sweets were being handed around with abandon.

Even the Right Reverend John MacCollie deigned to take off his dog collar before slipping into his bed that night.

Na Ordaighean - The Communions

comanaiche - communicants

curamach - the converted

Eaglais nan Eoin - church of the birds

geata iarran - the iron gate

crub - bent down

Each na Cnaimhan – 'the bones' horse

Balaich 'Houdie - the Shoudie boys (brothers)

Madainn mhat a' Mhinister, De tha a dhith oribh? - Good morning, Minister. What do you want?

Dha riribh, a'dhaoine - indeed, people

curam - conversion

midgies - rubbish bins / dykes - walls (Scots)

BILLY DUBH

It was a strange sight to see two huge golden eagles circling the Beinn low above *Taigh 'Houdie*. Equally strange was the fact that the people in the village below, mindful of the great birds' presence, were not in the least perturbed, which they certainly would have been in the past. Then, the sound of gunshot and the hysterical cry of '*Iolaire*' would have filled the air. Possibly they remembered how an eagle had played an important role in ridding the village of a killer mink, not so long ago. The great birds landed at the top of a *feannaig* beside *Taigh 'Houdie*, and the Shoudie 'boys' and their animal friends could only marvel at the majestic sight of two golden eagles approaching them with a waddling gait, reminiscent of a capercaillie, if you ever saw one. If any of the observers felt like smiling then the great beak and talons, not to mention the camera-like flicker of their wild eyes, persuaded them otherwise. Here in front of them stood Gilleasbuig of Beinn Bhragair and a young male eagle, who was introduced to the company as Ailpein. Gilleasbuig approached Iain 'Houdie, perhaps too close for comfort, and addressed him in heavily accented Lewis Eaglese. "Mr. Maclennan, your understanding of animals is legend in these parts, and it is because of this that we are here today." At this he unfolded his mighty wings to reveal a passenger clinging to the feathered neck of this awesome bird. It was a pigeon, thin and scrawny, unlike the large, plump specimens inhabiting the woods. Iain 'Houdie could see that one of the pigeon's wings was trailing, possibly fractured. That was why Gilleasbuig had brought the pigeon over to Dalmore, hoping that the Shoudie Boys could help. The bird was a racing pigeon en route from Thurso to Edinburgh, but strong easterly winds had greatly altered its course and the bird was found injured at Tom an Eoin near Beinn Bhragair. Gilleasbuig said that his name was Billy Dubh (well, that's how it sounded like to him), but Billy insisted that his second name was 'Doo', with the emphasis on the 'oo', as in 'too'.

Billy: "My name, as recorded in official documents at the Edinburgh Dovecote, is William Doo. I am a racing pigeon nowadays but before that I had a very unusual career. My lineage goes back a long way, to France, my mother told me. There was in the Mortonhall district of Edinburgh a unique group of 'doocots' where the resident pigeons were employed in a very old business indeed. We were carrier pigeons who were trained to carry messages between people and places. Everything depended on our well known homing instinct, used so often during wars, but the Mortonhall pigeons were involved in a more romantic and pleasing way. Specifically, we carried love letters between people, the lovesick and the lovelorn. We worked every day of the year, not just St. Valentine's Day. Rupie helped Billy down from off his own eagle 'nest' and a comfortable corner was found for him near the fire. Iain 'Houdie had already arranged with Seoras to drive him and the injured pigeon over to the vet's surgery in Stornoway.

Iain 'Houdie: "Billy Dubh or Billy Doo, we'll have to take you to the veterinary surgeon in Stornoway, who will see to your injured wing". The vet was a kindly old gentleman who had treated quite a few hens, some ducks and a grey parrot belonging to a Dutch seaman, but never a pigeon. With the use of a splint and some tape, the vet was positive that the wing would heal within a short time. As this was an unusual case, whose history amused him greatly, the vet said that there would be no charge.

Billy was very happy that he had come across such kindness here on the Island of Lewis. He was given some corn seed and a small saucer of water. So-Sally and Rupie were amused as Billy seemed to toss more seeds about him, than he consumed. Stowlia reminded them that this was no different from the behaviour of the hens at feeding time.

Billy's wing healed and there was no reason now for him to hang about Dalmore. The thought of leaving this idyll of a place, leaving all his new found friends made Billy very sad. Iain 'Houdie picked up on this, and asked his brother Murdo if a place could be found for Billy on *Lot a' Houdie.* Murdo said that Billy Dubh was welcome to stay as long as he wished - forever, if he had a mind to. Small tears of happiness formed on Billy's beak, as Soho, Rupie and Stowlia moved closer to embrace the latest member of *Taigh 'Houdie -* Billy Dubh, *Calman Sitheil.*

Seoras built a dovecote for Billy which was second to none. In all Edinburgh, where pigeon fancying was strong, Billy knew of no dovecote that could match the one which Seoras built. Billy was ecstatic with joy.

Rupie: "Billy, tell me. When you were flying about carrying these love letters, did you carry the paper messages in your beak? Didn't you suffer from 'lock beak' and did the paper not get wet from the drooling?"

Billy: "No, not in my beak! Around my neck I wore a fine silk ribbon, to which was attached a very small silver cylinder, into which the paper message was placed and the top closed. When we were out flying on these love missions, we weren't aware of the gear around our necks. At the receiving end, the message would be removed and read. If there was to be a reply, we often got a small feed of corn, a message would be attached, and we were released from whence we came. It was a good system but the telephone more or less did away with it. The telephone is faster, but far less romantic, and for the shy or the tongue-tied, the pigeon post was sans pareil".

Soho: "Was that French you spoke just now, Billy?"

Billy: "I think it was. This happens from time to time, and I never know why."

Soho: "Didn't you say that your ancestral pigeons came from France?"

Billy: "That's what Mother always maintained."

Soho had been thinking about Billy and his past involvement in a very specialised branch of the pigeon post. He asked Murdo about it, who was the village postman, but Murdo knew nothing about an equivalent service offered by the General Post Office. The Post Office did deliver Valentine cards but I don't think pigeons were involved.

Soho: "Billy, do you think you could carry messages again, here in Lewis? I take it that you intend to stay here with us in Dalmore!"

Billy: "I am staying here and, of course, carrying messages is not something a pigeon like me forgets."

Soho: "I think you would be in great demand. There are many spinsters and bachelors in the district, who are possibly too shy to make a move on their own but on paper can be quite bold in stating their case. There are many lovelorn souls around here, Billy, who would use your services. In Upper Carloway and Garenin alone, there are enough clients to keep you flying for months at a time. Shawbost would keep you going for years to come."

Seoras fashioned a beautiful little mahogany cylinder to carry the love notes and Mairi, his wife, fashioned a narrow tweed band for round Billy's neck. The love enterprise was ready to be launched. Small adverts were placed in the 'sheds' in Carloway, and Coinneach Uilleam even displayed an advert in his post office. The charge was six pence per letter, and moneys would be collected each Friday night by Stowlia or

Fancy. Billy was in his element again but on two occasions he was blown off course as the winds here on the west coast can be hard work for a wee Edinburgh doo. There was one young man from Ceann a-Staigh nan Ghearranan (inner Garenin) who spent a fortune on pigeon post, with excellent results he maintained. It has to be said that love was in the air and there was a surge in betrothals among persons you would never have thought of.

On a day off (and did he need it), Billy, Iain 'Houdie and the Dalmore Crew took a walk down to the *traigh*. There was a family staying in a large tent by the *allt* and, on the way back, greetings were exchanged. The people were from France, and were amazed at Iain's ability to interpret for this disparate collection of animals. He introduced them one by one, but when he mentioned Billy Doo, the French woman smiled.

French Lady: "That is a very sweet name, Billy, mon petit. It sounds exactly like the phrase we have in French – 'billet doux' which is a love letter, literally a 'soft, sweet letter' ".

Well, Billy could hardly believe what the woman had said, and everyone cheered.

Billy: "My mother was right about my French ancestry. My name is Love Letter, and my French ancestors were probably in the business of carrying messages long ago. Imagine finding out about 'billet doux' here in Dalmore!"

Iolaire – Eagle

Lot a' Houdie - the Shoudie croft

Calman Sitheil – Peaceful Dove

An Latha a' Thainig a Bhanrigh
(A Royal Visit)

It would be the summer of 1956, and there was much excitement surrounding the visit of the Royal Family to the Western Isles. Elizabeth, the young queen, had been crowned a mere three years earlier and here she was visiting some of the most distant islands in her realm. With her on board the Royal Yacht Britannia were her husband Prince Philip, her children, Charles and Anne, and other royal personages. Tomorrow they would be in Stornoway, and many islanders would turn out to see them in person, the visit being an 'occasion', rather than any demonstration of loyalty to the crown. From the time of the Lords of the Isles, and through the Jacobite Risings, Lewis never had much time for kings. But this young queen had captured the hearts of her people, and the Lewis folk were no exception.

The people and animals in Dalmore were, in a small way, excited about the Queen's visit. It's not everyone who would give up a full day at the hay or the corn to visit the town to stand for long periods among large crowds with no guarantee of a glimpse of the royal party. Others felt that a day like tomorrow might never happen again in Lewis during their lifetime. The four dogs, Stowlia, Fancy, Jura and Fred had made arrangements for a lift to town with Archie Bones at No. 10. Archie had one of those Bedford Dormobiles so beloved of the whalers when they hit the island during periods of leave from South Georgia. The cats were not fussed about the royal visit and kept saying things like "A cat can look at a queen, anytime". This was a cause of much hilarity, especially when

Victoria repeated this sentence in a cut-glass BBC accent. The dogs did not share in their humour, principally because they hadn't the faintest idea what the cats were on about. Fred kept repeating to himself "A cat can look at a queen", but he too, apart from the obvious, was quite confused. As he looked at each cat in turn, hoping for a clue to this riddle, Fred's gaze fixed on Victoria, haughty and with a curious thin smile on her face. She proceeded to regale the assembled company with the following 'poem' which one felt was really for Fred's benefit.

> *"Pussycat, Pussycat where have you been*
>
> *I've been to London to see the Queen*
>
> *Pussycat, Pussycat what did you there*
>
> *I frightened a little mouse from under her chair"*

All the cats fell about in paroxysms of laughter, belly-up with their *spogs* flailing about in the air. The dogs felt uneasy as this was a very strange situation indeed. Here in front of them was a group of demented cats, caterwauling with gusto, oblivious to the effect they might be having on their audience. Here we had So-Sally, Rupie, Filax, Guinness, Tigger, Vicky, Tom and Kenny Iceland strangely transformed in front of their eyes. Within the space of minutes, their feline friends took on the mantle of crazed creatures. This really spooked Wee Fred who had only ever seen one or two cats together, hissing or pissing in the back court of a Glasgow tenement. In the city sustained laughter like this, for no apparent reason, has a special name. Those involved are said to 'have the bonk' and as they tire, the least cackle from one, can bring back the 'bonk' again in a communal explosion of laughter. There are some other expressions similar to this. One that comes to mind is when a woman or animal is said 'to have the smit'.

This happens when one woman is holding a friend's newborn baby and becomes broody or, as it were, 'smitten' by an overwhelming desire for a child herself. Fred was fairly sure that the cats did not have the 'smit' (certainly not Old Tom and Kenny). Having the 'bonk' was bad enough. In time, the cats slowly regained their composure to the relief of all present. But Fred seemed determined to pursue the supposed relation between cats and the Queen. There were raised eyebrows and some head shakes among the other dogs. One felt that some of them may have been familiar with the doggerel espoused by the Lady Victoria. But not Fred.

Fred: "Of course a cat can look at a queen, but so too can a dog or anything with two eyes. So what's the big deal and why do you find it funny?"

Victoria: "A dog can look at a queen, Fred, but it doesn't say that in the saying 'A cat can look at a queen'. So there you have it. There must be a good reason why a cat was chosen over dogs, horses or sheep. I'll admit it's strange and funny when you think about it. Just accept it, Fred, and don't get yourself in a lather."

Fred just had to bite the bullet, as they say, on this one.

Fred: "Now, lady, who was this pussycat who left her friends only to pop up in London in the royal apartments of the Queen? Did this clever cat go there on spec, or was she answering a royal summons. After a long and dangerous journey to London, she somehow avoids the attentions of Her Majesty's guards, only to scare one poor bloody mouse from under her chair. No wonder you lot were almost dead laughing at your catpal's heroics. The least he could do was to toy with the mouse for a while before delivering the coup de grace (French, for children present.) Chasing a mouse away only invites it to return. Now Vicky, tell me the story behind the story of the pussycat and the Queen. I'm all ears Big Fluffy!"

Victoria: "Fred, Fred, you darling boy! It's only a nursery rhyme which parents recite to their children. There never was a real cat, or a mouse in the Queen's rooms in London. It is just a bit of fun. When we cats saw you taking the story about the 'Pussycat and the Queen' so literally and seriously, we could not contain ourselves from laughter. I am sorry, Dear Boy - just a jolly jape - a bit of feline fun, one might say."

Fred didn't think it at all funny, but the Wee Man gave a wan smile, hoping to hide his embarrassment. As Fred moved away, the cats knew that they had hurt his pride and must somehow make amends. Vicky was upset, and realised that her 'bit of fun' was someone else's pain. She didn't mean that to happen, but happen it did.

It was obvious that the cats would not now be going to see the Queen, only the dogs. Fred's good humour was restored and he was excited at the prospect of today's outing to Stornoway. There were large crowds in the centre of the town to see the royal procession of cars as they slowly passed by. The leading car, as you'd expect, contained the Queen and, this being a sunny day, had its top down. Prince Philip was driving, looking relaxed and cheerful. The Queen's sister, Princess Margaret Rose, followed in a Land Rover and everyone declared that she was a young princess of exceptional beauty. The Dalmore boys, pushing forward and peering through people's legs, had an excellent view of proceedings. They were sure that as they passed, Charles and Anne, the Queen's children gave our friends a special wave. There was no doubt that a reception would be held for the royal party in the Town Hall, or perhaps the Queen had invited the Provost and leading councillors to the Britannia for drinks and canapés. The crowds were breaking up, and the small flags and bunting were now looking a bit sad along the 'royal route.'

Stowlia, Fancy, Jura and Fred were a little tired now and climbed down the steps of the harbour at South Beach Street. There' they bathed their *spogs* in the salt water as they had taken a bit of a bashing in the crowds. Ah, ecstasy - pure and simple. Sammy, the resident harbour seal barked a greeting to them. Suddenly, they noticed a beautiful white launch coming across from Cuddy Point in their direction. It turned out to be a tender from the Britannia with four RN sailors aboard and standing in the prow were Charles and Anne and a couple of wee brown dogs. A young sailor said that the four Dalmore dogs had been invited to join the royal children and some more dogs on board the Royal Yacht. It seems that Stowlia and Co. had caught the royals' notice as they turned into Cromwell Street. The Queen said that it was nice to see loyal canine subjects in the crowd. In fact, she couldn't recall it happening before. Philip laughed and said that Her Majesty was grateful that there were no cats in the crowds. Philip quietly said that Lilibet (that's what he called the Queen) did not like cats that much. Fred wished that Iain 'Houdie was present so that he could pursue the topic of cats with the Queen. Bowls containing bits of lobster and salmon were put before our dogs, nothing short of the ambrosia eaten by the ancient gods! Before they left, they were assembled to sit in front of this flight of stairs which led to the upper deck. Then the Queen and Princess Anne led out about twenty dogs and had them sit in three rows. God, these were Welsh corgis and this was a choir of Welsh corgis assembled to entertain their guests from Dalmore. The Queen took over the baton, and the corgis gave renditions of 'Cwm Rhondda', 'Land of My Fathers' and, surprisingly, 'Hey, Big Spender'. Jura and Fred had seen choirs of Welsh corgis on the Sunday 'Dogs of Praise' programme on television and knew that, unless they left now, they could be there for a long time. You see, where you have two or more Welsh dogs brought together then that constitutes a choir and you can be held there for bloody hours!

On leaving, the Queen invited her loyal Scots dogs to visit her again sometime in the future.

Fred made up a new rhyme for the occasion:

> *"Puppy-dog, Puppy-dog where have you been,*
>
> *I've been to Stornoway to see the Queen,*
>
> *Puppy-dog, puppy-dog what did you there,*
>
> *I ate lobster and salmon next to her chair."*

"I'll have to see if Victoria knows *this* nursery rhyme? She can teach it to the other cats."

THE KIDNEY STONE

Jura, the black labrador, was in the mood for adventure, nothing too taxing mind you, just something different. "What kind of adventure did you have in mind?" asked Stowlia (*Cu 'Houdie*). "Well, back home, I and my best friend Solas would build a den in the depths of the Erskine woods in the springtime and this was a grand place to get away from it all. We could spend all day there, returning home only when hunger or sleep beckoned. I'm sure that you and Fancy must know of a place like this in Dalmore that would suit us all". "Jura, there are certainly no woods here, as you know, but a *bothan* or an old *airigh* might serve your purpose." said Stowlia. After giving some thought to Jura's proposal, it was Fancy, using Kenny Iceland's local knowledge, who made the following suggestion.

Fancy: "Just outside the village gate, high above the Mullach Beag, there are the ruined walls of an old dwelling, which date from around 1830 (Seoras says). It is an area of rock, interspersed with finely cropped green grass, beloved of sheep. This eminence is called Carnan Dubhagan which translates as The Cairn of the Kidneys, and Jura, before you ask, I don't know why it's called that! There are superb views from this high point, taking in the whole village, with commanding views of the Dalmore road along most of its length. It would be an ideal centre from which to launch your 'adventures'. Let's tell the gang and see what they think."

The gang thought about it and said that it wasn't a bad idea (faint praise, you might say) and resolved to visit the 'Kidney Stone' later that day. "*Rupie, na faighnich air Jura carson a ha feum againn air an aite seo - Dubhagan dha-riribh*" said Soho a little forcefully. (Rupie, don't ask Jura why we need this place - Kidneys, indeed). When it was revealed that the Kidney Stone was 250 feet above the road, Victoria, ever the diva, baulked at the idea. She maintained that her beautiful blue-cream coat would all be matted with disgusting oily peat and tangled in heather assuming, that is, she ever made it to the top. She added that an adventure could just as easily be conducted at sea level, or possibly a few feet above. Still, for her pal Jura (the 'poor dear') she did sign up. Fancy offered her a coalie-back to the top if she ever felt the need.

The whole team arrived at the 'Kidneys' to assess the site and to discuss what was required to build a den. Soho had told 'An 'Houdie of the gang's plans (Jura's actually) for Carnan Dughagan, realising that a lot of human input would be required to see their plans through. Iain Shoudie suggested that Domhnull Glass and Iain Mac na Cnamhan would be willing to help in this endeavour. Donald and John were up in Dalmore as they were every summer, Donald from Renfrew and John from London. These two young lads were so proud at being asked to help build an 'adventure centre' for their friends and they liked the 'new' name for an old *bothan*. Little were they to know that Jura had sown the seeds that flowered into 'adventure centres', across *an taobh siar* (the West Side) and even in Shawbost. Seoras provided the little wood and stone (and the technical advice) which would be needed to convert the bothan at Carnan Dughagan into a comfortable den for the Dalmore Gang. It had a wood and turf roof and the interior consisted of three apartments, whose walls were stone-built. Donald and John would occupy the room at the entrance, where a fire could be set when they were in residence. The boys would make occasional visits to supply some victuals, except for rabbit which those inveterate hunters, Tom Warrener and Kenny Iceland, could supply "ad nauseum" (these were Victoria's words). Actually the Gang would be grateful for rabbit because it was not usual fare in Dalmore homes.

The Kidney Stone was a great den, better than any Jura had seen in her neck of the woods. Even Lady Victoria was impressed but she kept in mind how any adventure starting here might entail a return climb of 250 feet. Still, Fancy had promised to be there for her. It didn't take the second sight for Fancy to read Vicky's mind. Guinness and Tigger were saying that coming up to Dalmore was adventure enough for them and that this idea of Jura's (of all people) was frankly surprising. Wee Fred was always game for anything new and he recalled his excitement and pride the day they caught and dispatched that mink. "Listen, gi'e Jura a bre'k. Our Dalmore cousins might just enjoy something a wee bit different, and that gang hut sounds just the job. Dick Whittington's cat had an adventurous spirit and people are still talking about him! We will only get out of this, what we put in." (That's what they said in the shipyards.)

In truth, the Dalmore Gang normally had plenty of opportunities for 'adventures' and with all the time to do so. The Dubhagan, by its location, allowed them to recce parts of Dalmore they wouldn't normally inhabit and it brought the gang together, cats and dogs, in joint activities. Well, that was the theory anyway and, if all else failed, they would be left with a super gang hut where they could retire from humanity, for short periods at least.

Donald and John arrived at The Dubhagan with various comestibles and a bag of peats (Where from? Don't ask!). They had with them some fishing rods and tackle and announced that they had a mind to catch some trout for supper. "Will we really get some trout?" enquired Tigger. "Of course you will" said London John in his usual booming voice. "We all shall have trout this very day" he boomed, with all the assurance of a London parliamentarian. John had great stories to tell and

Donald at times thought they were as amazing as *'An 'Houdie's*. They were big stories, fresh with the imprint of the capital.

They were all there, including the normally reticent Tom Warrener and Kenny Iceland, tramping down over the road at the Mullach Beag, heading for the Leathad Riabhach and Loch Langavat. This is one of the larger lochs in the area, whose Norse name means 'long lake'. There are quite a few lochs in Lewis with this name. In the fishing party there were two boys, who would do the fishing, and nine cats and four dogs to support them in this their first adventure from the Kidney Centre. Catching fish on Loch Langavat was difficult but the ones that took the fly were generally of a good size. It was hot and there was the first hint of midges. A whole hour had elapsed with only a few 'tickles' on the lines and one decent bite, according to London John. Some of the Dalmore Crew couldn't stay awake and had fallen asleep in the shade of a small *bruach*. The adventure had proved too much for them! Fred lay with his front *spogs* over his eyes but he was awake and listening to the lapwings' call in the distance, 'pee-wee, pee-wee'. He smiled when Victoria exclaimed, "This is so, so exciting - must repeat this adventure again!". Unbeknown to her, a dense cloud of midges was forming just above her head.

Suddenly, Donald had a fish on his line. The rod was bending in all directions and the fish, a brown trout, was leaping out of the water in a great show of acrobatics. Donald played the fish carefully all the way to the side of the loch, where John grabbed it throwing it up onto a heather bank. When it was weighed later in Seoras' workshop, it was two ounces short of two pounds. Donald was really happy as this was by far the biggest trout he had ever caught. The happiest 'person' there was Jura the labrador - her first adventure had been a success! In all, two smaller trout brought the tally to three which were roasted on the peat fire at the Dubhagan.

Strangely, that same cloud of midges had followed Vicky all the way from Loch Langavat and was hovering above her like an avenging angel.

After adventures would come rest periods of a couple of days, not long enough for some. Coincidentally it rained during this first period, not the kind which causes corrugated iron to rattle like a kettle drum but that fine rain which licks your face so gently, while seeking out every crevice in your *clo' guernsey.* Donald and John were in the 'anteroom' tending the fire using some 'borrowed' peats. It was very cosy in the Dughagan and sleep was catching up with the gang, replete after a lunch of rabbit. Forty winks later, they were refreshed and looking for some entertainment. Soho and Rupie caught Donald's eye gesturing towards London John. "John, I'm sure our friends would like to hear one of your amazing stories," said Donald.

London John: "Last summer I was training at the White City Track in London doing sprints and starts, when these two athletes approached with a request. Would I be prepared to run a leg of a mile race in a training session where we would set a fast pace for the last runner. I was to run the last leg taking over the pacing from the other two. Going round the last bend I looked over my left shoulder to see no one there but passing me on the other side was this tall lean man overtaking me with the speed of a gazelle. I literally could not see him now for the dust he left behind. These guys were in a different league to me but it was later that I realised that the tall lean man, who had passed me on that final bend, was a certain Dr. Roger Bannister who, at Oxford on the 6th of May 1954 ran the mile in under four minutes with the now famous time of 3 mins 59.4 secs."

What a story, a truly amazing story!

"This guy is unbelievable," said Fred. "You are so right," said Victoria, with a long wink and a fixed smile on her face.

Fred, Jura and Guinness particularly loved the novelty of eating and sleeping within the walls of Bothan Dughagan. They were in the innermost chamber, which had a small window through which shafts of light were thrown into relief by the blue peat smoke. They loved it there. The Shoudie animals, Soho, Rupie, Stowlia, thought there was little difference between here and the *taigh dubh* they normally inhabited, although it was a bit smaller. Kenny Iceland thought this an ideal base for future forays into the hills. He would speak to Tom Warrener about this.

On another day, Donald arranged for the young adventurers to have a game of football down on the old *leas* on Shonnie's croft, No.1 down by the *traigh* overlooking the cemetery. This *leas* dated from the time of the 'old people' (1780 - 1840) whose occupation of Dalmore was entirely located at the *machair*, which was very fertile. Now, of course, it was an area of close-cropped grass (sheep again), perfect for football once the area had been cleared of '*cac an caoraich*'. The sheep had been grazing here for months and had left a good bit of themselves behind! Victoria was at pains to state that since she was not taking part in the football, she would not spending hours cleaning up after sheep. "Why can't they bury it, like all cats do?".

The game got under way with a ball devised by Donald, not very large and made from Harris wool thread. Stowlia proved useful in goals and Fancy crossed some beautiful balls on to the head of wee Fred.

Soho and Rupie both raised their *spogs* to stop play - they saw a hearse drawing up at Taigh a' Bhoer and a great crowd of men gathering up the road, stretching beyond Taigh Dhomhnull Chalum. The coffin was transferred to an *eilitriom*, a wooden platform known as a 'bier' in English. The coffin is carried from here all the way to the graveside, with a succession of men moving forward to take their turn with the *eilitriom*. It is a moving sight to behold. No woman ever went to burials, even at the funeral of a husband. After the burial was over, none of the gang were in the mood to return to their game of football - another day, perhaps.

Donald (Domhnull Glass) actually spent four years of his childhood (1939 - 1943) in Dalmore, away from the threat of bombing in Renfrew. He stayed with his two aunts, Peigi and Dollag, and his grandfather, Old Bodach Glass' in the *taigh dubh* at No. 5 Dalmore. You will understand that, in these days, few vehicles ever came into the village, the exception being the hearses which would arrive at the Dalmore Cemetery at fairly regular intervals.

Donald, speaking only Gaelic, had to return to Renfrew in time for his first year at school. One day my mother noticed Donald staring out of the front window of our tenement house on Inchinnan Road, which overlooked a road junction busy with all kinds of buses, vans and cars. Mother asked Donald what he was looking at. After a short pause, Donald turned round and said,

"A Mhathair, nach eagalach nan thiodhlacadhean anns an aite seo." - Mother, there's an awful lot of burials in this place!

> *Cu 'Houdie* - the Shoudie dog
>
> *bothan* – bothy; *airidh* – shieling
>
> *bruach* – river bank; *leas* - small enclosed field

MacCollie Returns to Cardonald

School reunions are not always what we imagine them to be. We harbour sentimental thoughts about our fellow alumni and imagine them to be larger and older versions of how we saw them, all those years ago. Reunions, if they have to be arranged, should take place within the first twenty years of leaving school but not after that.

A favourite with some is the 'Class of '54' type reunion, an idea which has come from America like so many other things. The Class of '54 involves all the pupils who started their first year at school with you in 1954. I knew of an old friend of mine, Robert, who was invited to his Class of '03 school reunion dinner in a large hotel in Edinburgh. This was to be a 50th anniversary reunion, the first time most of these people had seen or heard of any of their 'old school friends' bar a few. For our old friend, it is easy to compute that the reunion of '03 took place last year in 1953 and that he would be around 11 years of age when he started secondary school in 1903. So, if you're still with me and your arithmetic is holding, it is obvious that Robert was 64 years of age when he entered the portals of that grand hotel in Edinburgh. What he expected, goodness alone knows.

What he saw was something entirely different. Before entering the reception room proper, Robert was handed his name badge by an ancient man, bald and lean, whose name meant nothing to Robert now, nor for that matter 50 years ago. With a handshake of welcome, and a weak smile, my friend passed through 'on the other side.' Holding his drink, he started to navigate his way through this throng of long forgotten names and faces. People would approach him to ask quite openly,

without demurring "Who are you, and do I know you?".
Robert felt like saying "Read the bloody name plate" but of
course he didn't. Here was a collection of grey hair, blue hair,
no hair, people with cocktail sticks, others with walking
sticks and the whole atmosphere replete with the smell of eau
de cologne and moth balls. People were peering closely at the
names on lapels, hoping to find someone to hold on to,
someone to talk to, a person they might have remembered
from the distant past. They quietly moved away with
him/her, as if it were their first morning with their new pal in
the school playground all these years ago. Robert had a
terrible premonition that he was attending a future
Christmas party at his own eventide home. He panicked at
the Hogarthian scene before him and left as soon as he could,
without causing offence. A 50 year anniversary reunion only
happens once in a life time and for some it is once too often.
It is an intimation of one's mortality which can be a
frightening thing.

The Right Reverend John MacCollie had risen early that
morning and was fully dressed as he prepared a simple
breakfast for himself in the kitchen of the manse in Doune,
Carloway. The postie had left three letters on the hall table.
"Is that a new collar you've got on?" asked the postman as he
left. MacCollie barked once in affirmation, thinking it
pointless to tell the man that it was a new clerical collar of
the best quality. However, *'An 'Houdie* would understand, and
what a boon that was when his services were called upon to
mediate between man and beast. You will remember that Big
MacCollie took the *curam* at the same time as his master all
these years back during the great 'revival' (or awakening) that
had swept through the island. His master had entered the
ministry and Doune was held up as a truly unique place
where one man and his dog occupied the same manse house
in two branches of the established church. John MacCollie
was handed one of the letters, which he could not read nor

understand and which his master could not translate for him. Told that the letter was from Glasgow, John became very excited and he determined to make his way to Dalmore to have Iain 'Houdie look it over.

MacCollie handed his letter to *'An 'Houdie* (to be accurate, it was passed from mouth to hand) and sat down on his haunches, tail wagging in excitement. He straightened his new dog collar with a *spog* and watched Iain's face as he read the letter. Finally Iain 'Houdie sat down beside him and said, "Well, a' Mhinistear, this will be a surprise, for sure. This letter is from the staff at the Cardonald Dog and Cat Home in Glasgow, inviting you to the first ever reunion of former alumni (whatever that is) in Glasgow at the end of September. They go on to say that, for obvious reasons, the number of guests must be restricted and in that regard they are looking to invite those that have made their mark in the animal world. A similar reunion will be held for the cats who started their lives in Cardonald."

At the end of September, John MacCollie travelled to Glasgow by train and Macbrayne (wee joke), accompanied by *'An 'Houdie*, who would intercede on his behalf, and Fred, the wee Glasgow dog, who would connect with the 'keelie dugs' (as he said) using the approved greetings of 'Big Man' or 'Wee Man'. A bit of a swagger and a good deal of attitude were important when confronted by the baying hounds of the South Side Team. Fred and Big Eck had a long-standing respect for one another. Fred called Eck 'Big Man', and Eck called Fred the 'Wee Man'. Thus honour and respect were mutually satisfied. Big Eck was of course the leader of the South Side Team which Fred knew controlled the Cardonald area.

Reunion day arrived and the Cardonald Home was spick and span for the occasion. Iain 'Houdie accompanied John to the venue and they were astonished to know that each famous alumnus was announced at the door. "Right Reverend John MacCollie, former Moderator of the Animal Church in Scotland, now ministering to our people on the Isle of Lewis. John was of the Class of '49. Welcome John." There was applause, but many eyes were fixed on *'An 'Houdie* whose presence was strange, to say the least. What was he doing here, among the great and the good of the dog world?

Over a beautiful meal, MacCollie got to know many of his fellow alumni. Bill was a black labrador, very like Jura, but, in truth, he thought they all looked the same anyway! Bill was a guide dog for a young lady, born blind. He was very skilled and it could be hard work depending on what the young lady was doing. It had its benefits and people were very kind. With the young lady, he was allowed into shops, cinemas and various other places where an unaccompanied dog could not go. Then there was Maisie, a cross collie, who, she said, was a 'sniffer' dog and worked along with the police and the fire brigade. John thought that all dogs did a bit of sniffing but to land a job sniffing, well! "It's not something *I'd* care to mention in polite company" he told *'An 'Houdie*. There were dogs who saved lives, dogs who could bark out answers to arithmetic problems employed by the banks and a beautiful standard poodle who had a large repertoire of songs, which saw her perform in the Five Past Eight Show at the Alhambra with Jimmy Logan and Stanley Baxter. She went under the name of Fifi Lamarr. She even persuaded our minister that he'd feel cooler and more comfortable if he removed his dog collar - and he did! In the company of so many dogs, Iain's presence here was of growing interest. Many had seen Iain and MacCollie in conversation and it wasn't long before *'An 'Houdie*'s secret was out. This was amazing - a person who could talk to all animals and understand them. As you can imagine, he was feted by the alumni who spoke as if they'd never get another chance to speak to a human being on equal terms.

Iain and John MacCollie were met by Fred outside the Cardonald Home. Fred gave them a guided tour of Glasgow's south side, ending up at Water Row beside the Govan Ferry. There, in numbers, were the South Side Team with Big Eck at the front. Eck asked if the Reverend MacCollie would give him and his boys a blessing which our minister felt would not be amiss, under the circumstances. Passengers off the ferry were amazed at the sight of perhaps thirty dogs, all with their heads bowed, listening to the barkings of a large black and white collie.

There was one final surprise in this amazing week. Some time later, another letter arrived at the Doune manse for Big John. He hurried down to Dalmore with this letter to have *'An 'Houdie* take a look. Iain's face said it all. This was a letter from Stanley Baxter to say that his friend, Fifi Lamaar, was sending her warmest greetings to the Rt. Rev. MacCollie. He was, she added, an imposing figure and a fine Highland dog, whose company she was blessed to keep. She did say that he didn't need to wear his dog collar at all times and she looked forward to them meeting in the not so distant future. The assembled group on *leathad 'Houdie* clapped and cheered and, although John was a bit embarrassed, Fred noticed a smile breaking on that bonnie, sonsie, face of his. Donnachadh Spagach, the church precentor, noticed a marked difference in his minister's demeanour. John was now easy going and happy as the day was long. Duncan was happy for his friend who went to Glasgow fairly often now, on church business of course.

Fifi Lamaar Travels To See MacCollie

It was a summer's evening in early August at around 9 o'clock when the Loch Seaforth came alongside Pier Number One in Stornoway. The boat was full to capacity and there was a buzz of excitement among its passengers. A large throng of relatives and friends had gathered on the quay. The tired but happy families were beginning to descend the gangway, assisted by the strong hands of the dockers. The sweet smell of peat smoke and the gentle lilt of Gaelic brought back memories of their island youth. *"Bha na duine bho tir mor a' tilleadh dhachaigh." - The people from the mainland were returning home.*

Suddenly there was a hush among the assembled crowd. Donald Alex, who was carrying luggage across the pier, turned round to see what might be amiss. There at the top of the gangway stood this magnificent black creature who was, as it were, posing for some unseen cameras. Here stood this tall, elegant 'standard' poodle, whose curly coat had been cut in the most amazing way, reminiscent it seemed of the way tall hedges are shaped in the gardens of fine houses. They call it the art of 'topiary'. This female had teeth of incredible whiteness and eyelashes as long as the bristles of a scrubbing brush. She had a pink ribbon fashioned as a bow atop her head and the most dazzling collar of diamante on leather.

"An e cu na caora ha sinn air neo an Donas Dubh?" shouted Donald Alex to a work colleague - *Is that a dog or a sheep or the Devil?* There were few on that quay who had ever seen or heard of a standard poodle, except perhaps those making their way to Matheson Road. But people were thrilled to see this exquisite lady moving like one of those fabulous horses of

the Spanish Riding School. Slowly she made her way to the buses parked on South Beach Street. It was then that one realised that the lady in charge of her was the lady five steps behind.

Lewis had witnessed the arrival of a very special personage, Miss Fifi Lamaar from Glasgow, whose name would be engraved on the memory of people on this island for years to come. Miss Lamaar and partner obviously knew which bus to board as they alighted the blue bus destined for Carloway. The 'Magaran' helped them on board and, carrying their fine leather cases, he found them seats at the rear of the bus. A crowd of Stornoway children were now gathered below the window at which Fifi sat. They were entranced at the sight of this exquisite creature and waved and cheered as the Carloway bus moved off. Fifi responded with a beautiful smile and waved a bejewelled *spog* in the manner of Her Majesty.

It began to rain as the bus made its way across the Barvas moor. Fifi and her companion, Isobel, looked forlornly out of the misted-up windows, looking for evidence of a living creature. Apart from the distant cry of a sheep, there were only heather clad moors, giant boulders and small lochs dotted across the landscape. Isobel could see that Fifi looked worried, if not a little afraid, and putting her arm around her, she whispered consoling words in her ear. Fifi might not understand what Isobel was saying but there was no doubt of the love behind these words.

After reaching the village of Barvas, the rain had stopped and the red rays of the setting sun fell upon the faces of the passengers. Fifi's spirits rose as she saw the lights go on in the houses. Children, gathered beside a small shop, waved at the people in the bus as it passed. Up the road a bit, the bus came to a standstill, as a group of cows were slowly making their way home for milking. As the bus slowly made its way through various villages, it would stop at times to let whole families of Gaels off to be met by their *cairdean*. Tears, and tears of laughter, would see the Magaran put the cases and boxes down by the croft gate. A half crown often made its way into a pocket in his bib overall.

Fifi had formed a picture in her mind of this countryside and only after delving into the recesses of her memory did she make the connection. Stanley Baxter used to read the Broons to her during breaks in rehearsal and her favourite stories would see the entire Broons family at their 'but an' ben' in the country. This was as near to that as one was likely to get. This was a unique place but very different from her home at Charing Cross Mansions in Glasgow, which she shared with Isobel.

It was now darker and the headlights of the bus picked out sheep with their lambs, many lying down on the road where it is said they benefit from the heat absorbed during the day. At Beinn Ghuidalum, overlooking the village of Dalbeg, a large part of that hill had been excavated in successive quarrying operations. The large number of lorries and various machines would suggest that Beinn Ghuidalum was working at full tilt at present. The darkness within the bus and the drone of its engine had lulled Fifi into a pleasant reverie. She instinctively knew that the journey which had begun at Queen Street Station this morning at 6am must now be near an end.

 At that moment, the Magaran announced that they were now at Carloway Bridge and that this was the terminus (he didn't use that word, exactly). He was saying that this was as far as he and his bus was going. "Is this near Doune Carloway" asked Isobel. "No, lady, this is Knock Carloway. Doune Carloway is a couple of miles further on past Chiribhig, but this bus doesn't go there". Fifi whispered something in Isobel's ear. "Sir, would it be possible to hire this bus as a taxi with you as driver of course? We could then get to Doune Carloway?". "Ah, well now. That is an unusual request but being as it is dark, and late, I'm sure something can be arranged" said the Magaran. "Do you have in mind an address there?". "Yes," said Isobel. "it's the Church of Scotland manse house in Doune". The Magaran was Free Church, but this was business. More half-crowns would be exchanged before the 'taxi' reached the gate leading up to the Doune manse. The Magaran led the way to the front door, where he deposited the ladies' luggage, before making a timely retreat back to the bus. There were lights on in the two rooms either side of the front door but the heavy drapes inside the windows were only partially closed.

 The moment had arrived and, with Fifi's nose maintaining pressure on Isobel's back, there would be no going back. Isobel stretched her arm to the wrought iron bell-pull and, pulling hard, the sounds that followed might have wakened the good people of Doune, if not Hell itself. The bell or bells pealed for a long time, or so it seemed to Isobel. The movement of shadows cast by the lights in the room suggested that someone, or something, was stirring in that house. *"Co tha aig an doras aig an uair seo?"* - *Who's at the door at this hour?* could be heard quite clearly, but these words were lost on the ladies outside. Shortly, the door opened and silhouetted in the hallway was this tall, powerfully built man. This was the Reverend Kenneth Graham, the minister residing in the Church of Scotland manse at Doune Carloway. What the Reverend Graham saw on the other side of the threshold struck him with awe and disbelief. In front of him stood a woman dressed in gypsy garb and tethered to her was this very large black beast with pink ribbons in its hair and a collar sparkling bright in the hall light. The reverend gentleman was very confused when Isobel made their introductions. "Sir, let me introduce myself and my friend to you. I am Miss Isobel Craig and this is Miss Fifi Lamaar, theatrical personages from Glasgow. I regret descending on you at this late hour, but Miss Lamaar is here at the invitation of her close friend, the Reverend John MacCollie, whose acquaintance she made a while back at the Cardonald Reunion in Glasgow. We believe he resides here with you." Fifi revealed her full set of brilliant white teeth and gave a rapid flutter of her long black eye lashes. The Reverend Graham was by now apoplectic and summoning his last reserves, he called out in a booming voice, *MACCOLLIE!!!*

Big John MacCollie appeared at the top of the stairs, a bit unsteady and bleary-eyed as if he had just emerged from a sleep (which he had). He gave a high pitched strangled bark, very unlike the deep growl his congregation were used to. Told he had visitors, John started down the stairs. He couldn't believe his eyes. There in front of him was the most beautiful creature he had ever seen. Fifi and John could not hide their love, which Isobel knew about but which was all news to John's master, the Reverend Graham. "Come now," said he, "Let us all come through to the sitting room, where the peat fire is burning warmly. Perhaps someone can tell me what's going on. What do you say, *Iain,'a bhalaich*" - *John, my boy*. John couldn't say anything except to bark very quietly. Isobel might be able to explain the present situation but for a fuller account the interpretative skills of *'An 'Houdie* would be needed. John and Fifi's tails were wagging in a show of love. The Reverend Graham mused that tongues would be wagging before long.

They all went down to Dalmore to visit their friends in *taigh 'Houdie* where they received a warm welcome. The animals were amazed to see the Reverend MacCollie (it wasn't time for the communions) but his lady friend, Miss Lamaar, rendered them all speechless. A visit from the Queen could not have been more surprising. It was noted that John MacCollie had dispensed with his dog collar and sported very modern casual wear, which you could only buy in Glasgow. He was by Fifi's side as he introduced her and Isobel to each one there. Fred thought that Miss Fifi was a 'big darling' (a *brammer* in the local vernacular) and hoped that he too could find a beautiful curly cutie like Fifi. John assured the Wee Man that the poodle was a very popular dog out in Glasgow and that they come in all sizes and colours (well, black or white to be sure). For Fred, this news made leaving Dalmore a little easier to take.

Big John was now relaxed about being without his clerical collar, which at times felt like a burden to him. He seemed to have experienced a kind of rebirth which had imbued in him a new happiness, for which the beautiful Fifi could take much of the credit. Iain 'Houdie placed Fifi and John in front of the fire with his arms around their shoulders. He spoke to them (as only he could) about their future plans, and whether these involved living in Lewis or going off to Glasgow. Confiding in *'An 'Houdie*, they revealed that they had determined to live in Glasgow, where Fifi could continue her theatrical career and where John would probably find a charge in one of the many Animal Churches in the Glasgow area. Isobel would stay with them, of course.

The holidays were over now for both the people and their animals and they would return to the *tir mor*. For John it would be to start anew in the City of Glasgow, albeit with Fifi by his side. For Jura, Fred, Guinness and Victoria, home for them was Renfrew. Although everybody was sad at leaving Dalmore, they knew that they would return again. Iain 'Houdie spoke to the animals once more, and recited this little ditty, which brought a tear to some eyes.

When Big Fred Hill will come with the bus,

There will be no more winking again,

One more wink at Stornoway Quay,

And no more winking again.

One more wink at Kyle of Lochalsh,

And no more winking again,

And one more wink at Renfrew Cross,

And no more winking again.

I know, I know, but it did have some meaning for the cats and dogs!

cairdean – relatives

tir mor – the mainland

We hope you have enjoyed the *'Tails'*

now visit the website!

Soho and Rupie and friends have their own website
where you can leave comments and catch up with new
stories as they are written

www.dalmoretails.co.uk